The NECTAR OF INSTRUCTION

BOOKS by His Divine Grace
A. C. Bhaktivedanta Swami Prabhupāda

Bhagavad-gītā As It Is
Śrīmad-Bhāgavatam (completed by disciples)
Śrī Caitanya-caritāmṛta
Kṛṣṇa, the Supreme Personality of Godhead
Teachings of Lord Caitanya
The Nectar of Devotion
The Nectar of Instruction
Śrī Īśopaniṣad
Light of the Bhāgavata
Easy Journey to Other Planets
Teachings of Lord Kapila, the Son of Devahūti
Teachings of Queen Kuntī
Message of Godhead
The Science of Self-Realization
The Perfection of Yoga
Beyond Birth and Death
On the Way to Kṛṣṇa
Rāja-vidyā: The King of Knowledge
Elevation to Kṛṣṇa Consciousness
Kṛṣṇa Consciousness: The Matchless Gift
Kṛṣṇa Consciousness: The Topmost Yoga System
Perfect Questions, Perfect Answers
Life Comes from Life
The Nārada-bhakti-sūtra (completed by disciples)
The Mukunda-mālā-stotra (completed by disciples)
Geetār-gān (Bengali)
Vairāgya-vidyā (Bengali)
Buddhi-yoga (Bengali)
Bhakti-ratna-boli (Bengali)
Back to Godhead magazine (founder)

BOOKS compiled from the teachings of His Divine Grace
A. C. Bhaktivedanta Swami Prabhupāda after his lifetime

Search for Liberation
Bhakti-yoga, the Art of Eternal Love
The Journey of Self-Discovery
Dharma, the Way of Transcendence
The Hare Kṛṣṇa Challenge
Renunciation Through Wisdom
A Second Chance
Beyond Illusion and Doubt
Civilization and Transcendence
Spiritual Yoga
The Laws of Nature
The Quest for Enlightenment

The Nectar of Instruction

An authorized English Presentation of
Śrīla Rūpa Gosvāmī's
Śrī Upadeśāmṛta

with the original Sanskrit text,
roman transliterations, synonyms,
translations and elaborate purports by

His Divine Grace
A. C. Bhaktivedanta
Swami Prabhupāda
Founder-*Ācārya* of the International Society
for Krishna Consciousness

THE BHAKTIVEDANTA BOOK TRUST
LOS ANGELES • STOCKHOLM • MUMBAI • SYDNEY

Readers interested in the subject matter of this book
are invited by the International Society for
Krishna Consciousness to correspond with its Secretary
at one of the following addresses:

International Society for Krishna Consciousness
P.O. Box 341445
Los Angeles, California 90034, USA
Telephone: 1-800-927-4152 (inside USA);
1-310-837-5283 (outside USA)
e-mail: bbt.usa@krishna.com
web: www.krishna.com

The Bhaktivedanta Book Trust
P.O. Box 380,
Riverstone, NSW 2765
Australia

Previous printings: 530,000
Current printing, 2010: 50,000

Printed in China

ISBN 0-912776-85-4

CONTENTS

PREFACE

The Kṛṣṇa consciousness movement is conducted under the supervision of Śrīla Rūpa Gosvāmī. The Gauḍīya Vaiṣṇavas, or Bengali Vaiṣṇavas, are mostly followers of Śrī Caitanya Mahāprabhu, of whom the Six Gosvāmīs of Vṛndāvana are direct disciples. Therefore Śrīla Narottama Dāsa Ṭhākura has sung:

rūpa-raghunātha-pade ha-ibe ākuti
kabe hāma bujhaba se yugala-pīriti

"When I am eager to understand the literature given by the Gosvāmīs, then I shall be able to understand the transcendental loving affairs of Rādhā and Kṛṣṇa." Śrī Caitanya Mahāprabhu appeared in order to bestow upon human society the benediction of the science of Kṛṣṇa. The most exalted of all the activities of Lord Kṛṣṇa are His pastimes of conjugal love with the *gopīs*. Śrī Caitanya Mahāprabhu appeared in the mood of Śrīmatī Rādhārāṇī, the best of the *gopīs*. Therefore, to understand the mission of Lord Śrī Caitanya Mahāprabhu and follow in His footsteps, one must very seriously follow in the footsteps of the six Gosvāmīs—Śrī Rūpa, Sanātana, Bhaṭṭa Raghunātha, Śrī Jīva, Gopāla Bhaṭṭa and Dāsa Raghunātha.

Śrī Rūpa Gosvāmī was the leader of all the Gosvāmīs, and to guide our activities he gave us this *Upadeśāmṛta* (*The Nectar of Instruction*) to follow. As Śrī Caitanya Mahāprabhu left behind Him the eight verses known as *Śikṣāṣṭaka,* Rūpa Gosvāmī gave us the *Upadeśāmṛta* so that we may become pure Vaiṣṇavas.

In all spiritual affairs, one's first duty is to control his mind and senses. Unless one controls his mind and senses, one cannot make any advancement in spiritual life. Everyone within this material world is engrossed in the modes of passion and ignorance. One must promote himself to the platform of goodness, *sattva-guṇa,* by following the instructions of Rūpa Gosvāmī, and then everything concerning how to make further progress will be revealed.

Advancement in Kṛṣṇa consciousness depends on the attitude of the follower. A follower of the Kṛṣṇa consciousness movement should become a perfect *gosvāmī.* Vaiṣṇavas are generally known as *gosvāmīs.* In Vṛndāvana, this is the title by which the director of each temple is known. One who wants to become a perfect devotee of Kṛṣṇa must become a *gosvāmī. Go* means "the senses," and *svāmī* means "the master." Unless one controls his senses and mind, one cannot become a *gosvāmī.* To achieve the highest success in life by becoming a *gosvāmī* and then a pure devotee of the Lord, one must follow the instructions known as *Upadeśāmṛta,* which have been given by Śrīla Rūpa Gosvāmī. Śrīla

Rūpa Gosvāmī has given many other books, such as the *Bhakti-rasāmṛta-sindhu, Vidagdha-mādhava* and *Lalita-mādhava*, but the *Upadeśāmṛta* constitutes the first instructions for neophyte devotees. One should follow these instructions very strictly. Then it will be easier to make one's life successful. Hare Kṛṣṇa.

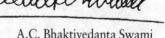

A.C. Bhaktivedanta Swami

September 20, 1975
Viśvarūpa-mahotsava
Kṛṣṇa-Balarāma Mandira
Ramaṇa-reti
Vṛndāvana, India

TEXT ONE

वाचो वेगं मनसः क्रोधवेगं
जिह्वावेगमुदरोपस्थवेगम् ।
एतान् वेगान् यो विषहेत धीरः
सर्वामपीमां पृथिवीं स शिष्यात् ॥१॥

vāco vegaṁ manasaḥ krodha-vegaṁ
jihvā-vegam udaropastha-vegam
etān vegān yo viṣaheta dhīraḥ
sarvām apīmāṁ pṛthivīṁ sa śiṣyāt

vācaḥ—of speech; *vegam*—the urge; *manasaḥ*—of the mind; *krodha*—of anger; *vegam*—the urge; *jihvā*—of the tongue; *vegam*—the urge; *udara-upastha*—of the belly and genitals; *vegam*—the urge; *etān*—these; *vegān*—urges; *yaḥ*—whoever; *viṣaheta*—can tolerate; *dhīraḥ*—sober; *sarvām*—all; *api*—certainly; *imām*—this; *pṛthivīm*—world; *saḥ*—that personality; *śiṣyāt*—can make disciples.

TRANSLATION

A sober person who can tolerate the urge to speak, the mind's demands, the actions of anger and the urges of the tongue, belly and genitals is qualified to make disciples all over the world.

PURPORT

In *Śrīmad-Bhāgavatam* (6.1.9-10) Parīkṣit Mahārāja placed a number of intelligent questions before Śukadeva Gosvāmī. One of these questions was: "Why do people undergo atonement if they cannot control their senses?" For instance, a thief may know perfectly well that he may be arrested for his stealing, and he may actually even see another thief arrested by the police, yet he continues to steal. Experience is gathered by hearing and seeing. One who is less intelligent gathers experience by seeing, and one who is more intelligent gathers experience by hearing. When an intelligent person hears from the lawbooks and *śāstras,* or scriptures, that stealing is not good and hears that a thief is punished when arrested, he refrains from theft. A less intelligent person may first have to be arrested and punished for stealing to learn to stop stealing. However, a rascal, a foolish man, may have the experience of both hearing and seeing and may even be punished, but still he continues to steal. Even if such a person atones and is punished by the government, he will again commit theft as soon as he comes out of jail. If punishment in jail is considered atonement, what is the benefit of such atonement? Thus Parīkṣit Mahārāja inquired:

dṛṣṭa-śrutābhyāṁ yat pāpaṁ
jānann apy ātmano 'hitam
karoti bhūyo vivaśaḥ
prāyaścittam atho katham

kvacin nivartate 'bhadrāt
kvacic carati tat punaḥ

TEXT ONE

prāyaścittam atho 'pārthaṁ
manye kuñjara-śaucavat

Parīkṣit Mahārāja compared atonement to an elephant's bathing. The elephant may take a very nice bath in the river, but as soon as it comes onto the bank, it throws dirt all over its body. What, then, is the value of its bathing? Similarly, many spiritual practitioners chant the Hare Kṛṣṇa *mahā-mantra* and at the same time commit many forbidden things, thinking that their chanting will counteract their offenses. Of the ten types of offenses one can commit while chanting the holy name of the Lord, this offense is called *nāmno balād yasya hi pāpa-buddhiḥ,* committing sinful activities on the strength of chanting the Hare Kṛṣṇa *mahā-mantra.* Similarly, certain Christians go to church to confess their sins, thinking that confessing their sins before a priest and performing some penance will relieve them from the results of their weekly sins. As soon as Saturday is over and Sunday comes, they again begin their sinful activities, expecting to be forgiven the next Saturday. This kind of *prāyaścitta,* or atonement, is condemned by Parīkṣit Mahārāja, the most intelligent king of his time. Śukadeva Gosvāmī, equally intelligent, as befitting the spiritual master of Mahārāja Parīkṣit, answered the King and confirmed that his statement concerning atonement was correct. A sinful activity cannot be counteracted by a pious activity. Thus real *prāyaścitta,* atonement, is the awakening of our dormant Kṛṣṇa consciousness.

Real atonement involves coming to real knowledge, and for this there is a standard process. When one follows a regulated hygienic process, he does not fall sick.

A human being is meant to be trained according to certain principles to revive his original knowledge. Such a methodical life is described as *tapasya.* One can be gradually elevated to the standard of real knowledge, or Kṛṣṇa consciousness, by practicing austerity and celibacy (*brahmacarya*), by controlling the mind, by controlling the senses, by giving up one's possessions in charity, by being avowedly truthful, by keeping clean and by practicing *yoga-āsanas.* However, if one is fortunate enough to get the association of a pure devotee, he can easily surpass all the practices for controlling the mind by the mystic *yoga* process simply by following the regulative principles of Kṛṣṇa consciousness—refraining from illicit sex, meat-eating, intoxication and gambling—and by engaging in the service of the Supreme Lord under the direction of the bona fide spiritual master. This easy process is being recommended by Śrīla Rūpa Gosvāmī.

First one must control his speaking power. Every one of us has the power of speech; as soon as we get an opportunity we begin to speak. If we do not speak about Kṛṣṇa consciousness, we speak about all sorts of nonsense. A toad in a field speaks by croaking, and similarly everyone who has a tongue wants to speak, even if all he has to say is nonsense. The croaking of the toad, however, simply invites the snake: "Please come here and eat me." Nevertheless, although it is inviting death, the toad goes on croaking. The talking of materialistic men and impersonalist Māyāvādī philosophers may be compared to the croaking of frogs. They are always speaking nonsense and thus inviting death to catch them. Controlling speech, however, does not mean self-imposed silence (the external process of *mauna*), as Māyāvādī philosophers think. Silence may appear helpful for some time, but ultimately it proves a failure. By contrast, the controlled speech advocated by Śrīla Rūpa Gosvāmī is the positive process of *kṛṣṇa-kathā*, engaging the speaking process in glorifying the Supreme Lord Śrī Kṛṣṇa. The tongue can thus glorify the name, form, qualities and pastimes of the Lord. The preacher of *kṛṣṇa-kathā* is always beyond the clutches of death. This is the significance of controlling the urge to speak.

The restlessness or fickleness of the mind (*mano-vega*) is controlled when one can fix his mind on the lotus feet of Kṛṣṇa. The *Caitanya-caritāmṛta* (*Madhya* 22.31) says:

kṛṣṇa—sūrya-sama; māyā haya andhakāra
yāhāṅ kṛṣṇa, tāhāṅ nāhi māyāra adhikāra

Kṛṣṇa is just like the sun, and *māyā* is just like darkness. If the sun is present, there is no question of darkness. Similarly, if Kṛṣṇa is present in the mind, there is no possibility of the mind's being agitated by *māyā's* influence. The yogic process of negating all material thoughts will not help. To try to create a vacuum in the mind is artificial. The vacuum will not remain. However, if one always thinks of Kṛṣṇa and how to serve Kṛṣṇa best, one's mind will naturally be controlled.

Similarly, anger can be controlled. We cannot stop anger altogether, but if we simply become angry with those who blaspheme the Lord or the devotees of the Lord, we control our anger in Kṛṣṇa consciousness. Lord Caitanya Mahāprabhu became angry with the miscreant brothers Jagāi and Mādhāi, who blasphemed and struck Nityānanda Prabhu. In His *Śikṣāṣṭaka* Lord Caitanya wrote, *tṛṇād api sunīcena taror api sahiṣṇunā:* "One should be humbler than the grass and more tolerant than the tree." One may then ask why the Lord exhibited His anger. The point is that one should be ready to tolerate all insults to one's own self, but when Kṛṣṇa or His pure devotee is blasphemed, a genuine devotee becomes angry and acts like fire against the offenders. *Krodha,* anger, cannot be stopped, but it can be applied rightly. It was in anger that Hanumān set fire to Laṅkā, but he is worshiped as the greatest devotee of Lord Rāmacandra. This means that he utilized his anger in the right way. Arjuna serves as another example. He was not willing to fight, but Kṛṣṇa incited his anger: "You must fight!" To fight without anger is not possible. Anger is controlled, however, when utilized in the service of the Lord.

As for the urges of the tongue, we all experience that the tongue wants to eat palatable dishes. Generally we should not allow the tongue to eat according to its choice, but should control the tongue by supplying *prasādam.* The devotee's attitude is that he will eat only when Kṛṣṇa gives him *prasādam.* That is the way to control the urge of the tongue. One should take *prasādam* at scheduled times and should not eat in restaurants or sweetmeat shops simply to satisfy the whims of the tongue or belly. If we stick to the principle of taking only *prasādam,* the urges of the belly and tongue can be controlled.

In a similar manner, the urges of the genitals, the sex impulse, can be controlled when not used unnecessarily. The genitals should be used to beget a Kṛṣṇa conscious child; otherwise they should not be used. The Kṛṣṇa consciousness movement encourages marriage not for the satisfaction of the genitals but for the begetting of Kṛṣṇa conscious children. As soon as the children are a little grown up, they are sent to our *gurukula* school, where they are trained to become fully Kṛṣṇa conscious devotees. Many such Kṛṣṇa conscious children are required, and one who is capable of bringing forth Kṛṣṇa conscious offspring is allowed to utilize his genitals.

When one is fully practiced in the methods of Kṛṣṇa conscious control, he can become qualified to be a bona fide spiritual master.

In his *Anuvṛtti* explanation of the *Upadeśāmṛta,* Śrīla Bhaktisiddhānta Sarasvatī Ṭhākura writes that our material identification creates three kinds of urges—the urge to speak, the urges or demands of the mind, and the demands of the body. When a living entity falls victim to these three types of urges, his life becomes inauspicious. One who practices resisting these demands or urges is called a *tapasvī,* or one who practices austerities. By such *tapasya* one can overcome victimization by the material energy, the external potency of the Supreme Personality of Godhead.

When we refer to the urge to speak, we refer to useless talking, such as that of the impersonal Māyāvādī philosophers, or of persons engaged in fruitive activities (technically called *karma-kāṇḍa*), or of materialistic people who simply want to enjoy life without restriction. All such talks or literatures are practical exhibitions of the urge to speak. Many people are talking nonsensically and writing volumes of useless books, and all this is the result of the urge to speak. To counteract this tendency, we have to divert our talking to the subject of Kṛṣṇa. This is explained in *Śrīmad-Bhāgavatam* (1.5.10–11):

na yad vacaś citra-padaṁ harer yaśo
jagat-pavitraṁ pragṛṇīta karhicit
tad vāyasaṁ tīrtham uśanti mānasā
na yatra haṁsā niramanty uśik-kṣayāḥ

"Those words which do not describe the glories of the Lord, who alone can sanctify the atmosphere of the whole universe, are considered by saintly persons to be like unto a place of pilgrimage for crows. Since the all-perfect persons are inhabitants of the transcendental abode, they do not derive any pleasure there."

tad-vāg-visargo janatāgha-viplavo
yasmin prati-ślokam abaddhavaty api
nāmāny anantasya yaśo 'ṅkitāni yat
śṛṇvanti gāyanti gṛṇanti sādhavaḥ

"On the other hand, that literature which is full of descriptions of the transcendental glories of the name, fame, forms, pastimes, etc., of the unlimited Supreme Lord is a different creation, full of transcendental words directed toward bringing about a revolution in the impious lives of this world's misdirected civilization. Such transcendental literatures, even though imperfectly composed, are heard, sung and accepted by purified men who are thoroughly honest."

The conclusion is that only when we talk about devotional service to the Supreme Personality of Godhead can we refrain from useless nonsensical talk. We should always endeavor to use our speaking power solely for the purpose of realizing Kṛṣṇa consciousness.

As for the agitations of the flickering mind, they are divided into two divisions. The first is called *avirodha-prīti,* or unrestricted attachment, and the other is called *virodha-yukta-krodha,* anger arising from frustration. Adherence to the philosophy of the Māyāvādīs, belief in the fruitive results of the *karma-vādīs,* and belief in plans based on materialistic desires are called *avirodha-prīti. Jñānīs, karmīs* and materialistic plan-makers generally attract the attention of conditioned souls, but when the materialists cannot fulfill their plans and when their devices are frustrated, they become angry. Frustration of material desires produces anger.

Similarly, the demands of the body can be divided into three categories—the demands of the tongue, the belly and the genitals. One may observe that these three senses are physically situated in a straight line, as far as the body is concerned, and that the bodily demands begin with the tongue. If one can restrain the demands of the tongue by limiting its activities to the eating of *prasādam,* the urges of the belly and the genitals can automatically be controlled. In this connection Śrīla Bhaktivinoda Ṭhākura says:

śarīra avidyā-jāla, jaḍendriya tāhe kāla,
jīve phele viṣaya-sāgare
tā'ra madhye jihvā ati, lobhamaya sudurmati,
tā'ke jetā kaṭhina saṁsāre

kṛṣṇa baḍa dayāmaya, karibāre jihvā jaya,
sva-prasāda-anna dila bhāi
sei annāmṛta khāo, rādhā-kṛṣṇa-guṇa gāo,
preme ḍāka caitanya-nitāi

"O Lord! This material body is a lump of ignorance, and the senses are a netw-ork of paths leading to death. Somehow or other we have fallen into the ocean of material sense enjoyment, and of all the senses the tongue is the most voracious and uncontrollable. It is very difficult to conquer the tongue in this world, but You, dear Kṛṣṇa, are very kind to us. You have sent this nice *prasādam* to help us conquer the tongue; therefore let us take this *prasādam* to our full satisfaction and glorify Your Lordships Śrī Śrī Rādhā and Kṛṣṇa and in love call for the help of Lord Caitanya and Prabhu Nityānanda."

There are six kinds of *rasas* (tastes), and if one is agitated by any one of them, he becomes controlled by the urges of the tongue. Some persons are attracted to the eating of meat, fish, crabs, eggs and other things produced by semen and blood and eaten in the form of dead bodies. Others are attracted by eating vegetables, creepers, spinach or milk products, but all for the satisfaction of the tongue's demands. Such eating for sense gratification—including the use of extra quantities of spices like chili and tamarind—is to be given up by Kṛṣṇa conscious persons. The use of pan, *haritakī,* betel nuts, various spices used in pan-making, tobacco, LSD, marijuana, opium, liquor, coffee and tea is indulged in to fulfill illicit demands. If we can practice accepting only remnants of food offered to Kṛṣṇa, it is possible to get free from *māyā's* victimization. Vegetables, grains, fruits, milk products and water are proper foods to offer to the Lord, as Lord Kṛṣṇa Himself prescribes. However, if one accepts *prasādam* only because of its palatable taste and thus eats too much, he also falls prey to trying to satisfy the demands of the tongue. Śrī Caitanya Mahāprabhu taught us to avoid very palatable dishes even while eating *prasādam*. If we offer palatable dishes to the Deity with the intention of eating such nice food, we are involved in trying to satisfy the demands of the tongue. If we accept the invitation of a rich man with the idea of receiving palatable food, we are also trying to satisfy the demands of the tongue. In the *Caitanya-caritāmṛta* (*Antya* 6.227) it is stated:

jihvāra lālase yei iti-uti dhāya
śiśnodara-parāyaṇa kṛṣṇa nāhi pāya

"That person who runs here and there seeking to gratify his palate and who is always attached to the desires of his stomach and genitals is unable to attain Kṛṣṇa."

As stated before, the tongue, belly and genitals are all situated in a straight line, and they fall into the same category. Lord Caitanya has said, *bhāla nā khāibe āra bhāla nā paribe:* "Do not dress luxuriously and do not eat delicious foods." (Cc. *Antya* 6.236)

Those who suffer from diseases of the stomach must be unable to control the urges of the belly, at least according to this analysis. When we desire to eat more than necessary, we automatically create many inconveniences in life. However, if we observe fasting days like Ekādaśī and Janmāṣṭamī, we can restrain the demands of the belly.

As far as the urges of the genitals are concerned, there are two—proper and improper, or legal and illicit sex. When a man is properly mature, he can marry according to the rules and regulations of the *śāstras* and use his genitals for begetting nice children. That is legal and religious. Otherwise, he may adopt many artificial means to satisfy the demands of the genitals, and he may not use any restraint. When one indulges in illicit sex, as defined by the *śāstras,* either by thinking, planning, talking about or actually having sexual intercourse, or by satisfying the genitals by artificial means, he is caught in the clutches of *māyā.* These instructions apply not only to householders but also to *tyāgīs,* or those who are in the renounced order of life. In his book *Prema-vivarta,* Chapter Seven, Śrī Jagadānanda Paṇḍita says:

vairāgī bhāi grāmya-kathā nā śunibe kāne
grāmya-vārtā nā kahibe yabe milibe āne

svapane o nā kara bhāi strī-sambhāṣaṇa
gṛhe strī chāḍiyā bhāi āsiyācha vana

yadi cāha praṇaya rākhite gaurāṅgera sane
choṭa haridāsera kathā thāke yena mane

bhāla nā khāibe āra bhāla nā paribe
hṛdayete rādhā-kṛṣṇa sarvadā sevibe

"My dear brother, you are in the renounced order of life and should not listen to talk about ordinary worldly things, nor should you talk about worldly things when you meet with others. Do not think of women even in dreams. You have accepted the renounced order of life with a vow that forbids you to associate with women. If you wish to associate with Caitanya Mahāprabhu, you must always remember the incident of Choṭa Haridāsa and how he was rejected by the Lord. Do not eat luxurious dishes or dress in fine garments, but always remain humble and serve Their Lordships Śrī Śrī Rādhā-Kṛṣṇa in your heart of hearts."

The conclusion is that one who can control these six items—speech, mind, anger, tongue, belly and genitals—is to be called a *svāmī* or *gosvāmī*. *Svāmī* means master, and *gosvāmī* means master of the *go,* or senses. When one accepts the renounced order of life, he automatically assumes the title of *svāmī*. This does not mean that he is the master of his family, community or society; he must be master of his senses. Unless one is master of his senses, he should not be called *gosvāmī,* but *go-dāsa,* servant of the senses. Following in the footsteps of the Six Gosvāmīs of Vṛndāvana, all *svāmīs* and *gosvāmīs* should fully engage in the transcendental loving service of the Lord. As opposed to this, the *go-dāsas* engage in the service of the senses or in the service of the material world. They have no other engagement. Prahlāda Mahārāja has further described the *go-dāsa* as *adānta-go,* which refers to one whose senses are not controlled. An *adānta-go* cannot become a servant of Kṛṣṇa. In *Śrīmad-Bhāgavatam* (7.5.30), Prahlāda Mahārāja has said:

matir na kṛṣṇe parataḥ svato vā
mitho 'bhipadyeta gṛha-vratānām

adānta-gobhir viśatāṁ tamisraṁ
punaḥ punaś carvita-carvaṇānām

"For those who have decided to continue their existence in this material world for the gratification of their senses, there is no chance of becoming Kṛṣṇa conscious, not by personal endeavor, by instruction from others or by joint conferences. They are dragged by the unbridled senses into the darkest region of ignorance, and thus they madly engage in what is called 'chewing the chewed.'"

TEXT TWO

अत्याहारः प्रयासश्च प्रजल्पो नियमाग्रहः ।
जनसङ्गश्च लौल्यं च षड्भिर्भक्तिर्विनश्यति ॥२॥

atyāhāraḥ prayāsaś ca
prajalpo niyamāgrahaḥ
jana-saṅgaś ca laulyaṁ ca
ṣaḍbhir bhaktir vinaśyati

ati-āhāraḥ—overeating or collecting too much; *prayāsaḥ*—overendeavoring; *ca*—and; *prajalpaḥ*—idle talk; *niyama*—rules and regulations; *āgrahaḥ*—too much attachment to (or *agrahaḥ*—too much neglect of); *jana-saṅgaḥ*—association with worldly-minded persons; *ca*—and; *laulyam*—ardent longing or greed; *ca*—and; *ṣaḍbhiḥ*—by these six; *bhaktiḥ*—devotional service; *vinaśyati*—is destroyed.

TRANSLATION

One's devotional service is spoiled when he becomes too entangled in the following six activities: (1) eating more than necessary or collecting more funds than required; (2) overendeavoring for mundane things that are very difficult to obtain; (3) talking unnecessarily about mundane subject matters; (4) practicing the scriptural rules and regulations only for the sake of following them and not for the sake of spiritual advancement, or rejecting the rules and regulations of the scriptures and working independently or whimsically; (5) associating with worldly-minded persons who are not interested in Kṛṣṇa consciousness; and (6) being greedy for mundane achievements.

PURPORT

Human life is meant for plain living and high thinking. Since all conditioned living beings are under the control of the Lord's third energy, this material world is designed so that one is obliged to work. The Supreme Personality of Godhead has three primary energies, or potencies. The first is called the *antaraṅga-śakti,* or the internal potency. The second is called the *taṭasthā-śakti,* or the marginal potency. The third is called the *bahiraṅga-śakti,* or the external potency. The living entities constitute the marginal potency, and they are situated between the internal and external potencies. Being subordinate as eternal servants of the Supreme Personality of Godhead, the *jīvātmās,* or atomic living entities, must remain under the control of either the internal or external potency. When they are under the control of the internal potency, they display their natural, constitutional activity—namely, constant engagement in the devotional service of the Lord. This is stated in the *Bhagavad-gītā* (9.13):

mahātmānas tu māṁ pārtha
daivīṁ prakṛtim āśritāḥ
bhajanty ananya-manaso
jñātvā bhūtādim avyayam

"O son of Pṛthā, those who are not deluded, the great souls, are under the protection of the divine nature. They are fully engaged in devotional service because they know Me as the Supreme Personality of Godhead, original and inexhaustible."

The word *mahātmā* refers to those who are broadminded, not cripple-minded. Cripple-minded persons, always engaged in satisfying their senses, sometimes expand their activities in order to do good for others through some "ism" like nationalism, humanitarianism or altruism. They may reject personal sense gratification for the sense gratification of others, like the members of their family, community or society—either national or international. Actually all this is extended sense gratification, from personal to communal to social. This may all be very good from the material point of view, but such activities have no spiritual value. The basis of such activity is sense gratification, either personal or extended. Only when a person gratifies the senses of the Supreme Lord can he be called a *mahātmā*, or broadminded person.

In the above-quoted verse from the *Bhagavad-gītā*, the words *daivīṁ prakṛtim* refer to the control of the internal potency, or pleasure potency, of the Supreme

Personality of Godhead. This pleasure potency is manifested as Śrīmatī Rādhārāṇī, or Her expansion Lakṣmī, the goddess of fortune. When the individual *jīva* souls are under the control of the internal energy, their only engagement is the satisfaction of Kṛṣṇa, or Viṣṇu. This is the position of a *mahātmā*. If one is not a *mahātmā*, he is a *durātmā*, or a cripple-minded person. Such mentally crippled *durātmās* are put under the control of the Lord's external potency, *mahāmāyā*.

Indeed, all living entities within this material world are under the control of *mahāmāyā*, whose business is to subject them to the influence of threefold miseries: *ādhidaivika-kleśa* (sufferings caused by the demigods, such as droughts, earthquakes and storms), *ādhibhautika-kleśa* (sufferings caused by other living entities like insects or enemies), and *ādhyātmika-kleśa* (sufferings caused by one's own body and mind, such as mental and physical infirmities). *Daiva-bhūtātma-hetavaḥ:* the conditioned souls, subjected to these three miseries by the control of the external energy, suffer various difficulties.

The main problem confronting the conditioned souls is the repetition of birth, old age, disease and death. In the material world one has to work for the maintenance of the body and soul, but how can one perform such work in a way that is favorable for the execution of Kṛṣṇa consciousness? Everyone requires possessions such as food grains, clothing, money and other things necessary for the maintenance of the body, but one should not collect more than necessary for his actual basic needs. If this natural principle is followed, there will be no difficulty in maintaining the body.

According to nature's arrangement, living entities lower on the evolutionary scale do not eat or collect more than necessary. Consequently in the animal kingdom there is generally no economic problem or scarcity of necessities. If a bag of rice is placed in a public place, birds will come to eat a few grains and go away. A human being, however, will take away the whole bag. He will eat all his stomach can hold and then try to keep the rest in storage. According to scriptures, this collecting of more than necessary (*atyāhāra*) is prohibited. Now the entire world is suffering because of it.

Collecting and eating more than necessary also causes *prayāsa*, or unnecessary endeavor. By God's arrangement, anyone in any part of the world can live very peacefully if he has some land and a milk cow. There is no need for man to move from one place to another to earn a livelihood, for one can produce food grains locally and get milk from cows. That can solve all economic problems. Fortunately, man has been given higher intelligence for the cultivation of Kṛṣṇa consciousness, or the understanding of God, one's relationship with Him, and the ultimate goal of life, love of God. Unfortunately, so-called civilized man, not caring for God realization, utilizes his intelligence to get more than necessary and simply eat to satisfy the tongue. By God's arrangement there is sufficient scope for the production of milk and grains for human beings all over the world, but instead of using his higher intelligence to cultivate God consciousness, so-called intelligent men misuse their intelligence to produce many unnecessary and unwanted things. Thus factories, slaughterhouses, brothels and liquor shops are opened. If people are advised not to collect too many goods, eat too much or work unnecessarily to possess artificial amenities, they think they are being advised to return to a primitive way of life. Generally people do not like to accept plain living and high thinking. That is their unfortunate position.

Human life is meant for God realization, and the human being is given higher intelligence for this purpose. Those who believe that this higher intelligence is meant to attain a higher state should follow the instructions of the Vedic literatures. By taking such instructions from higher authorities, one can actually become situated in perfect knowledge and give real meaning to life.

In *Śrīmad-Bhāgavatam* (1.2.9) Śrī Sūta Gosvāmī describes the proper human *dharma* in this way:

dharmasya hy āpavargyasya
nārtho 'rthāyopakalpate
nārthasya dharmaikāntasya
kāmo lābhāya hi smṛtaḥ

"All occupational engagements [*dharma*] are certainly meant for ultimate liberation. They should never be performed for material gain. Furthermore, one who is engaged in the ultimate occupational service [*dharma*] should never use material gain to cultivate sense gratification."

The first step in human civilization consists of occupational engagements performed according to the scriptural injunctions. The higher intelligence of a human being should be trained to understand basic *dharma*. In human society there are various religious conceptions characterized as Hindu, Christian, Hebrew, Mohammedan, Buddhist and so on, for without religion, human society is no better than animal society.

As stated above (*dharmasya hy āpavargyasya nārtho 'rthāyopakalpate*), religion is meant for attaining emancipation, not for getting bread. Sometimes human society manufactures a system of so-called religion aimed at material advancement, but that is far from the purpose of true *dharma.* Religion entails understanding the laws of God because the proper execution of these laws ultimately leads one out of material entanglement. That is the true purpose of religion. Unfortunately, people accept religion for material prosperity because of *atyāhāra,* or an excessive desire for such prosperity. True religion, however, instructs people to be satisfied with the bare necessities of life while cultivating Kṛṣṇa consciousness. Even though we require economic development, true religion allows it only for supplying the bare necessities of material existence. *Jīvasya tattva jijñāsā:* the real purpose of life is to inquire about the Absolute Truth. If our endeavor (*prayāsa*) is not to inquire about the Absolute Truth, we will simply increase our endeavor to satisfy our artificial needs. A spiritual aspirant should avoid mundane endeavor.

Another impediment is *prajalpa,* unnecessary talking. When we mix with a few friends, we immediately begin unnecessary talking, sounding just like croaking toads. If we must talk, we should talk about the Kṛṣṇa consciousness movement. Those outside of the Kṛṣṇa consciousness movement are interested in reading heaps of newspapers, magazines and novels, solving crossword puzzles and doing many other nonsensical things. In this fashion people simply waste their valuable time and energy. In the Western countries old men, retired from active life, play cards, fish, watch television and debate about useless socio-political schemes. All these and other frivolous activities are included in the *prajalpa* category. Intelligent persons interested in Kṛṣṇa consciousness should never take part in such activities.

Jana-saṅga refers to associating with persons not interested in Kṛṣṇa consciousness. One should strictly avoid such association. Śrīla Narottama Dāsa Ṭhākura has therefore advised us to live only in the association of Kṛṣṇa conscious devotees (*bhakta-sane vāsa*). One should always engage in the service of the Lord in the association of the Lord's devotees. Association with those engaged in a similar line of business is very conducive to advancement in that business. Consequently materialistic persons form various associations and clubs to enhance their endeavors. For example, in the business world we find such institutions as the stock exchange and chamber of commerce. Similarly, we have established the International Society for Krishna Consciousness to give people an opportunity to associate with those who have not forgotten Kṛṣṇa. This spiritual association offered by our ISKCON movement is increasing day by day. Many people from different parts of the world are joining this Society to awaken their dormant Kṛṣṇa consciousness.

Śrīla Bhaktisiddhānta Sarasvatī Ṭhākura writes in his *Anuvṛtti* commentary that too much endeavor to acquire knowledge on the part of mental speculators or dry philosophers falls within the category of *atyāhāra* (collecting more than needed). According to *Śrīmad-Bhāgavatam*, the endeavor of philosophical speculators to write volumes of books on dry philosophy devoid of Kṛṣṇa consciousness is entirely futile. The work of *karmīs* who write volumes of books on economic development also falls within the category of *atyāhāra.* Similarly, those who have no desire for Kṛṣṇa consciousness and who are simply interested in possessing more and more material things—either in the shape of scientific knowledge or monetary gain—are all included under the control of *atyāhāra.*

Karmīs labor to accumulate more and more money for future generations only because they do not know their future position. Interested only in getting more and more money for their sons and grandsons, such foolish persons do not even know what their position is going to be in the next life. There are many incidents that illustrate this point. Once a great *karmī* accumulated a vast fortune for his sons and grandsons, but later, according to his *karma,* he took his birth in a cobbler's house located near the building which in his previous life he had constructed for his children. It so happened that when this very cobbler came to his former house, his former sons and grandsons beat him with shoes. Unless the *karmīs* and *jñānīs* become interested in Kṛṣṇa consciousness, they will simply continue to waste their life in fruitless activities.

Accepting some of the scriptural rules and regulations for immediate benefit, as utilitarians advocate, is called *niyama-āgraha,* and neglecting the rules and regulations of the *śāstras,* which are meant for spiritual development, is called *niyama-agraha.* The word *āgraha* means "eagerness to accept," and *agraha* means "failure to accept."

By the addition of either of these two words to the word *niyama* ("rules and regulations"), the word *niyamāgraha* is formed. Thus *niyamāgraha* has a twofold meaning that is understood according to the particular combination of words. Those interested in Kṛṣṇa consciousness should not be eager to accept rules and regulations for economic advancement, yet they should very faithfully accept scriptural rules and regulations for the advancement of Kṛṣṇa consciousness. They should strictly follow the regulative principles by avoiding illicit sex, meat-eating, gambling and intoxication.

One should also avoid association with Māyāvādīs, who simply blaspheme Vaiṣṇavas (devotees). *Bhukti-kāmīs,* who are interested in material happiness, *mukti-kāmīs,* who desire liberation by merging into the existence of the formless Absolute (Brahman), and *siddhi-kāmīs,* who desire the perfection of mystic *yoga* practice, are classified as *atyāhārīs.* To associate with such persons is not at all desirable.

Desires to expand the mind by perfecting mystic *yoga,* merging into the existence of Brahman, or attaining whimsical material prosperity are all included within the category of greed (*laulya*). All attempts to acquire such material benefits or so-called spiritual advancement are impediments on the path of Kṛṣṇa consciousness.

Modern warfare waged between capitalists and communists is due to their avoiding the advice of Śrīla Rūpa Gosvāmī regarding *atyāhāra.* Modern capitalists accumulate more wealth than necessary, and the communists, envious of their prosperity, want to nationalize all wealth and property. Unfortunately the communists do not know how to solve the problem of wealth and its distribution. Consequently when the wealth of the capitalists falls into the hands of the communists, no solution results. Opposed to these two philosophies, the Kṛṣṇa conscious ideology states that all wealth belongs to Kṛṣṇa. Thus unless all wealth comes under the administration of Kṛṣṇa, there can be no solution to the economic problem of mankind. Nothing can be solved by placing wealth in the hands of the communists or the capitalists. If a hundred-dollar bill is lying on the street, someone may pick it up and put it in his pocket. Such a man is not honest. Another man may see the money and decide to let it remain there, thinking that he should not touch another's property. Although this second man does not steal the money for his own purposes, he is unaware of its proper use. The third man who sees the hundred-dollar bill may pick it up, find the man who lost it and deliver it to him. This man does not steal the money to spend for himself, nor does he neglect it and let it lie in the street. By taking it and delivering it to the man who has lost it, this man is both honest and wise.

Simply transferring wealth from capitalists to communists cannot solve the problem of modern politics, for it has been demonstrated that when a communist gets money, he uses it for his own sense gratification. The wealth of the world actually belongs to Kṛṣṇa, and every living entity, man and animal, has the birthright to use God's property for his maintenance. When one takes more than his maintenance requires—be he a capitalist or a communist—he is a thief, and as such he is liable to be punished by the laws of nature.

The wealth of the world should be used for the welfare of all living entities, for that is the plan of Mother Nature. Everyone has the right to live by utilizing the wealth of the Lord. When people learn the art of scientifically utilizing the Lord's property, they will no longer encroach upon one another's rights. Then an ideal society can be formed. The basic principle for such a spiritual society is stated in the first *mantra* of *Śrī Īśopaniṣad:*

īśāvāsyam idaṁ sarvaṁ
yat kiñca jagatyāṁ jagat
tena tyaktena bhuñjīthā
mā gṛdhaḥ kasya svid dhanam

"Everything animate or inanimate that is within the universe is controlled and owned by the Lord. One should therefore accept only those things necessary for himself, which are set aside as his quota, and should not accept other things, knowing well to whom they belong."

Kṛṣṇa conscious devotees know very well that this material world is designed by the complete arrangement of the Lord to fulfill all the necessities of life for all living beings, without their having to encroach upon the life or rights of one another. This complete arrangement affords the proper quota of wealth for everyone according to his real needs, and thus everyone may live peacefully according to the principle of plain living and high thinking. Unfortunately, materialists who have neither faith in the plan of God nor any aspiration for higher spiritual development misuse their God-given intelligence only to augment their material possessions. They devise many systems—such as capitalism and materialistic communism—to advance their material position. They are not interested in the laws of God or in a higher goal. Always anxious to fulfill their unlimited desires for sense gratification, they are conspicuous by their ability to exploit their fellow living beings.

When human society gives up these elementary faults enumerated by Śrīla Rūpa Gosvāmī (*atyāhāra*, etc.), all enmity will cease between men and animals, capitalists and communists, and so forth. In addition, all problems of economic or political maladjustment and instability will be solved. This pure consciousness is awakened by the proper spiritual education and practice offered scientifically by the Kṛṣṇa consciousness movement.

This Kṛṣṇa consciousness movement offers a spiritual community that can bring about a peaceful condition in the world. Every intelligent man should purify his consciousness and rid himself of the above-mentioned six hindrances to devotional service by taking wholehearted shelter of this Kṛṣṇa consciousness movement.

TEXT THREE

उत्साहान्निश्चयाद्धैर्यात् तत्तत्कर्मप्रवर्तनात् ।
सङ्गत्यागात्सतो वृत्तेः षड्भिर्भक्तिः प्रसिध्यति ॥३॥

utsāhān niścayād dhairyāt
tat-tat-karma-pravartanāt
saṅga-tyāgāt sato vṛtteḥ
ṣaḍbhir bhaktiḥ prasidhyati

utsāhāt—by enthusiasm; *niścayāt*—by confidence; *dhairyāt*—by patience; *tat-tat-karma*—various activities favorable for devotional service; *pravartanāt*—by performing; *saṅga-tyāgāt*—by giving up the association of nondevotees; *sataḥ*—of the great previous *ācāryas; vṛtteḥ*—by following in the footsteps; *ṣaḍbhiḥ*—by these six; *bhaktiḥ*—devotional service; *prasidhyati*—advances or becomes successful.

TRANSLATION

There are six principles favorable to the execution of pure devotional service: (1) being enthusiastic, (2) endeavoring with confidence, (3) being patient, (4) acting according to regulative principles [such as śravaṇaṁ kīrtanaṁ viṣṇoḥ smaraṇam—hearing, chanting and remembering Kṛṣṇa], (5) abandoning the association of nondevotees, and (6) following in the footsteps of the previous ācāryas. These six principles undoubtedly assure the complete success of pure devotional service.

PURPORT

Devotional service is not a matter of sentimental speculation or imaginative ecstasy. Its substance is practical activity. Śrīla Rūpa Gosvāmī, in his *Bhakti-rasāmṛta-sindhu* (1.1.11), has defined devotional service as follows:

anyābhilāṣitā-śūnyaṁ
jñāna-karmādy-anāvṛtam
ānukūlyena kṛṣṇānu-
śīlanaṁ bhaktir uttamā

"*Uttamā bhakti*, or unalloyed devotion unto the Supreme Personality of Godhead, Śrī Kṛṣṇa, involves the rendering of devotional service in a way that is favorable to the Lord. This devotional service should be free from any extraneous motive and devoid of fruitive *karma*, impersonal *jñāna* and all other selfish desires."

Bhakti is a sort of cultivation. As soon as we say "cultivation," we must refer to activity. Cultivation of spirituality does not mean sitting down idly for meditation, as some pseudo-*yogīs* teach. Such idle meditation may be good for those who have no information of devotional service, and for this reason it is sometimes recommended as a way to check distracting materialistic activities. Meditation means stopping all nonsensical activities, at least for the time being. Devotional service, however, not only puts an end to all nonsensical mundane activities, but also engages one in meaningful devotional activities. Śrī Prahlāda Mahārāja recommends:

śravaṇaṁ kīrtanaṁ viṣṇoḥ
smaraṇaṁ pāda-sevanam
arcanaṁ vandanaṁ dāsyaṁ
sakhyam ātma-nivedanam

The nine processes of devotional service are as follows:

1. hearing the name and glories of the Supreme Personality of Godhead
2. chanting His glories
3. remembering the Lord
4. serving the Lord's feet

5. worshiping the Deity
6. offering obeisances unto the Lord
7. acting as the Lord's servant
8. making friends with the Lord
9. surrendering oneself fully to the Lord

Śravaṇam, or hearing, is the first step in acquiring transcendental knowledge. One should not give aural reception to unauthorized persons, but should approach the proper person, as recommended in the *Bhagavad-gītā* (4.34):

tad viddhi praṇipātena
paripraśnena sevayā
upadekṣyanti te jñānaṁ
jñāninas tattva-darśinaḥ

"Just try to learn the truth by approaching a spiritual master. Inquire from him submissively and render service unto him. The self-realized soul can impart knowledge unto you because he has seen the truth."

It is further recommended in the *Muṇḍaka Upaniṣad, tad-vijñānārthaṁ sa gurum evābhigacchet:* "To understand that transcendental science, one must approach a bona fide spiritual master." Thus this method of submissively receiving transcendental confidential knowledge is not merely based on mental speculation. In this regard, Śrī Caitanya Mahāprabhu told Rūpa Gosvāmī:

brahmāṇḍa bhramite kona bhāgyavān jīva
guru-kṛṣṇa-prasāde pāya bhakti-latā-bīja

"In the course of traversing the universal creation of Brahmā, some fortunate soul may receive the seed of the *bhakti-latā,* the creeper of devotional service. This is all by the grace of *guru* and Kṛṣṇa." The material world is a place of confinement for the living entities, who are by nature *ānandamaya,* pleasure-seeking. They actually want to be free from the confinement of this world of conditional happiness, but not knowing the process of liberation, they are bound to transmigrate from one species of life to another and from one planet to another. In this way the living entities are wandering throughout the material universe. When by good fortune one comes in contact with a pure devotee and hears from him patiently, one begins to follow the path of devotional service. Such an opportunity is offered to a person who is sincere. The International Society for Krishna Consciousness is giving such a chance to humanity at large. If by fortune one takes advantage of this opportunity to engage in devotional service, the path of liberation immediately opens.

One should accept this opportunity to return home, back to Godhead, very enthusiastically. Without enthusiasm, one cannot be successful. Even in the material world one has to be very enthusiastic in his particular field of activity in order to become successful. A student, businessman, artist or anyone else who wants success in his line must be enthusiastic. Similarly, one has to be very enthusiastic in devotional service. Enthusiasm means action, but action for whom? The answer is that one should always act for Kṛṣṇa—*kṛṣṇārthākhila-ceṣṭā* (*Bhakti-rasāmṛta-sindhu*).

In all phases of life one has to perform devotional

activities under the direction of the spiritual master in order to attain perfection in *bhakti-yoga*. It is not that one has to confine or narrow one's activities. Kṛṣṇa is all-pervading. Therefore nothing is independent of Kṛṣṇa, as Kṛṣṇa Himself states in the *Bhagavad-gītā* (9.4):

mayā tatam idaṁ sarvaṁ
jagad avyakta-mūrtinā-
mat-sthāni sarva-bhūtāni
na cāhaṁ teṣv avasthitaḥ

"By Me, in My unmanifested form, this entire universe is pervaded. All beings are in Me, but I am not in them." Under the direction of the bona fide spiritual master, one has to make everything favorable for Kṛṣṇa's service. For example, at present we are using a dictaphone. The materialist who invented this machine intended it for businessmen or writers of mundane subject matters. He certainly never thought of using the dictaphone in God's service, but we are using this dictaphone to write Kṛṣṇa conscious literature. Of course, the manufacture of the dictaphone is wholly within the energy of Kṛṣṇa. All the parts of the instrument, including the electronic functions, are made from different combinations and interactions of the five basic types of material energy—namely, *bhūmi, jala, agni, vāyu* and *ākāśa*. The inventor used his brain to make this complicated machine, and his brain, as well as the ingredients, were supplied by Kṛṣṇa. According to the statement of Kṛṣṇa, *mat-sthāni sarva-bhūtāni:* "Everything is depending on My energy." Thus the devotee can understand that since nothing is independent of Kṛṣṇa's energy, everything should be dovetailed in His service.

Endeavor executed with intelligence in Kṛṣṇa consciousness is called *utsāha,* or enthusiasm. The devotees find the correct means by which everything can be utilized in the service of the Lord (*nirbandhaḥ kṛṣṇa-sambandhe yuktaṁ vairāgyam ucyate*). The execution of devotional service is not a matter of idle meditation but practical action in the foreground of spiritual life.

These activities must be executed with patience. One should not be impatient in Kṛṣṇa consciousness. Indeed, this Kṛṣṇa consciousness movement was started single-handedly, and in the beginning there was no response, but because we continued to execute our devotional activities with patience, people gradually began to understand the importance of this movement, and now they are eagerly participating. One should not be impatient in discharging devotional service, but should take instructions from the spiritual master and execute them with patience, depending on the mercy of *guru* and Kṛṣṇa. The successful execution of Kṛṣṇa conscious activities requires both patience and confidence. A newly married girl naturally expects offspring from her husband, but she cannot expect to have them immediately after marriage. Of course, as soon as she is married she can attempt to get a child, but she must surrender to her husband, confident that her child will develop and be born in due time. Similarly, in devotional service surrender means that one has to become confident. The devotee thinks, *avaśya rakṣibe kṛṣṇa:* "Kṛṣṇa will surely protect me and give me help for the successful execution of devotional service." This is called confidence.

As already explained, one should not be idle but should be very enthusiastic about executing the regulative principles—*tat-tat-karma-pravartana.* Neglect of the regulative principles will destroy devotional service. In this Kṛṣṇa consciousness movement there are four basic regulative principles, forbidding illicit sex, meat-eating, gambling and intoxication. A devotee must be very enthusiastic about following these principles. If he becomes slack in following any of them, his progress will certainly be checked. Śrīla Rūpa Gosvāmī therefore recommends, *tat-tat-karma-pravartanāt:* "One must strictly follow the regulative principles of *vaidhī-bhakti.*" In addition to these four prohibitions (*yama*), there are positive regulative principles (*niyama*), such as the daily chanting of sixteen rounds on *japa-mālā* beads. These regulative activities must be faithfully performed with enthusiasm. This is called *tat-tat-karma-pravartana,* or varied engagement in devotional service.

Furthermore, in order to be successful in devotional service one must give up the association of undesirable people. This includes *karmīs, jñānīs, yogīs* and other nondevotees. Once Śrī Caitanya Mahāprabhu was asked by one of His householder devotees about the general principles of Vaiṣṇavism, as well as the general routine activities of a Vaiṣṇava, and Śrī Caitanya Mahāprabhu immediately replied, *asat-saṅga-tyāga,—ei vaiṣṇava-ācāra:* "Characteristically, a Vaiṣṇava is one who gives up the association of worldly people, or nondevotees." Śrīla Narottama Dāsa Ṭhākura has therefore recommended, *tāṅdera caraṇa sevi bhakta-sane vāsa:* one has to live in the company of pure devotees and execute the regulative principles laid down by the previous *ācāryas,* the Six Gosvāmīs (namely, Śrī Rūpa Gosvāmī, Śrī Sanātana Gosvāmī, Śrī Jīva Gosvāmī, Śrī Raghunātha Dāsa Gosvāmī, Śrī Gopāla Bhaṭṭa Gosvāmī and Śrī Raghunātha Bhaṭṭa Gosvāmī). If one lives in the association of devotees, there is little chance of associating with nondevotees. The International Society for Krishna Consciousness is opening many centers just to invite people to live in the company of devotees and practice the regulative principles of spiritual life.

Devotional service means transcendental activities. On the transcendental platform there is no contamination by the three modes of material nature. This is called *viśuddha-sattva,* the platform of pure goodness, or goodness free from contamination by the qualities of passion and ignorance. In this Kṛṣṇa consciousness movement we require everyone to rise early in the morning, by four o'clock., and attend *maṅgala-ārati,* or morning worship, then read *Śrīmad-Bhāgavatam,* perform *kīrtana,* and so forth. Thus we hold continuous activities in devotional service twenty-four hours daily. This is called *sato vṛtti,* or following in the footsteps of the previous *ācāryas,* who expertly filled every moment of time with Kṛṣṇa conscious activities.

If one strictly follows the advice given in this verse by Śrīla Rūpa Gosvāmī—namely, being enthusiastic, being confident, being patient, giving up the association of unwanted persons, following the regulative principles and remaining in the association of devotees—one is sure to advance in devotional service. In this regard Śrīla Bhaktisiddhānta Sarasvatī Ṭhākura remarks that the cultivation of knowledge by philosophical speculation, the collection of mundane opulence by the advancement of fruitive activities, and the desire for *yoga-siddhis,* material perfections, are all contrary to the principles of devotional service. One has to become thoroughly callous to such nonpermanent activities and turn his intention instead to the regulative principles of devotional service. According to the *Bhagavad-gītā* (2.69):

yā niśā sarva-bhūtānāṁ
tasyāṁ jāgarti saṁyamī
yasyāṁ jāgrati bhūtāni
sā niśā paśyato muneḥ

"What is night for all beings is the time of awakening for the self-controlled; and the time of awakening for all beings is night for the introspective sage."

Engagement in the devotional service of the Lord is the life and soul of the living entity. It is the desired goal and supreme perfection of human life. One has to become confident about this, and one also has to be confident that all activities other than devotional service—such as mental speculation, fruitive work or mystic endeavor—will never yield any enduring benefit. Complete confidence in the path of devotional service will enable one to attain his desired goal, but attempting to follow other paths will only succeed in making one restless. In the Seventh Canto of *Śrīmad-Bhāgavatam* it is stated: "One must be calmly convinced that those who have given up devotional service to engage in severe austerities for other purposes are not purified in their minds, despite their advanced austerities, because they have no information of the transcendental loving service of the Lord."

It is further stated in the Seventh Canto: "Although mental speculators and fruitive actors may perform great austerities and penances, they still fall down because they do not have information about the lotus feet of the Lord." The devotees of the Lord, however, never fall down. In the *Bhagavad-gītā* (9.31), the Supreme Personality of Godhead assures Arjuna, *kaunteya pratijānīhi na me bhaktaḥ praṇaśyati*: "O son of Kuntī, declare it boldly that My devotee never perishes."

Again in the *Bhagavad-gītā* (2.40) Kṛṣṇa says:

nehābhikrama-nāśo 'sti
pratyavāyo na vidyate
svalpam apy asya dharmasya
trāyate mahato bhayāt

"In this endeavor there is no loss or diminution, and a little advancement on this path can protect one from the most dangerous type of fear."

Devotional service is so pure and perfect that once one has begun it, one is forcibly dragged to ultimate success. Sometimes a person will give up his ordinary material engagements and out of sentiment take shelter of the lotus feet of the Supreme Lord and thus begin the preliminary execution of devotional service. Even if such an immature devotee falls down, there is no loss on his part. On the other hand, what is the gain of one who executes the prescribed duties according to his *varṇa* and *āśrama* but does not take to devotional service? Although a fallen devotee may take his next birth in a low family, his devotional service will nonetheless resume from where it left off. Devotional service is *ahaituky apratihatā:* it is not the effect of any mundane cause, nor can it be terminated by any mundane cause or permanently curtailed by any material interruption. Therefore a devotee should be confident about his engagement and should not be very interested in the activities of the *karmīs, jñānīs* and *yogīs.*

There are certainly many good qualities among fruitive actors, philosophical speculators and mystic *yogīs,* but all good qualities automatically develop in the character of a devotee. No extraneous endeavor is needed. As confirmed by *Śrīmad-Bhāgavatam* (5.18.12), all the good qualities of the demigods progressively become manifest in one who has developed pure devotional service. Because a devotee is not interested in any material activity, he does not become materially contaminated. He is immediately situated on the platform of transcendental life. However, one who engages in mundane activity—be he a so-called *jñānī, yogī, karmī,* philanthropist, nationalist or whatever—cannot attain the higher stage of *mahātmā.* He remains a *durātmā,* or cripple-minded person. According to the *Bhagavad-gītā* (9.13):

mahātmānas tu māṁ pārtha
daivīṁ prakṛtim āśritāḥ
bhajanty ananya-manaso
jñātvā bhūtādim avyayam

"O son of Pṛthā, those who are not deluded, the great souls, are under the protection of the divine nature.

They are fully engaged in -devotional service because they know Me as the Supreme Personality of Godhead, original and inexhaustible."

Since all the devotees of the Lord are under the protection of His supreme potency, they should not deviate from the path of devotional service and take to the path of the *karmī, jñānī* or *yogī*. This is called *utsāhān niścayād dhairyāt tat-tat-karma-pravartanāt,* enthusiastically executing the regulative activities of devotional service with patience and confidence. In this way one can advance in devotional service without hindrance.

TEXT FOUR

ददाति प्रतिगृह्णाति गुह्यमाख्याति पृच्छति ।
भुङ्क्ते भोजयते चैव षड्विधं प्रीतिलक्षणम् ॥४॥

dadāti pratigṛhṇāti
guhyam ākhyāti pṛcchati
bhuṅkte bhojayate caiva
ṣaḍ-vidhaṁ prīti-lakṣaṇam

dadāti—gives charity; *pratigṛhṇāti*—accepts in return; *guhyam*—confidential topics; *ākhyāti*—explains; *pṛcchati*—enquires; *bhuṅkte*—eats; *bhojayate*—feeds; *ca*—also; *eva*—certainly; *ṣaṭ-vidham*—six kinds; *prīti*—of love; *lakṣaṇam*—the symptoms.

TRANSLATION

Offering gifts in charity, accepting charitable gifts, revealing one's mind in confidence, inquiring confidentially, accepting prasādam and offering prasādam are the six symptoms of love shared by one devotee and another.

PURPORT

In this verse Śrīla Rūpa Gosvāmī explains how to perform devotional activities in the association of other devotees. There are six kinds of activities: (1) giving charity to the devotees, (2) accepting from the devotees whatever they may offer in return, (3) opening one's mind to the devotees, (4) inquiring from them about the confidential service of the Lord, (5) honoring *prasādam,* or spiritual food, given by the devotees, and (6) feeding the devotees with *prasādam.* An experienced devotee explains, and an inexperienced devotee learns from him. This is *guhyam ākhyāti pṛcchati.* When a devotee distributes *prasādam,* remnants of food offered to the Supreme Personality of Godhead, in order to maintain our spirit of devotional service we must accept this *prasādam* as the Lord's grace received through the pure devotees. We should also invite pure devotees to our home, offer them *prasādam* and be prepared to please them in all respects. This is called *bhuṅkte bhojayate caiva.*

Even in ordinary social activities, these six types of dealings between two loving friends are absolutely necessary. For instance, when one businessman wishes to contact another businessman he arranges a feast in a hotel, and over the feast he openly expresses what he wishes to do. He then inquires from his business friend how he should act, and sometimes presents are exchanged. Thus whenever there is a dealing of *prīti*, or love in intimate dealings, these six activities are executed. In the previous verse, Śrīla Rūpa Gosvāmī advised that one should renounce worldly association and keep company with the devotees (*saṅga-tyāgāt sato vṛtteḥ*). The International Society for Krishna Consciousness has been established to facilitate these six kinds of loving exchanges between devotees. This Society was started single-handedly, but because people are coming forward and experiencing the give-and-take policy, the Society is now expanding all over the world. We are glad that people are donating very liberally to the development of the Society's activities, and people are also eagerly accepting whatever humble contribution we are giving them in the shape of books and magazines dealing strictly with the subject matter of Kṛṣṇa consciousness. We sometimes hold Hare Kṛṣṇa festivals and invite life members and friends to participate in the feasting by accepting *prasādam*. Although most of our members come from the higher rungs of society, they nonetheless come and take whatever little *prasādam* we are able to offer them. Sometimes the members and supporters inquire very confidentially about the methods of performing devotional service, and we try to explain this. In this way our Society is successfully spreading all over the world, and the intelligentsia of all countries is gradually appreciating our Kṛṣṇa conscious activities. The life of the Kṛṣṇa conscious society is nourished by these six types of loving exchange among the members; therefore people must be given the chance to associate with the devotees of ISKCON because simply by reciprocating in the six ways mentioned above an ordinary man can fully revive his dormant Kṛṣṇa consciousness. In the *Bhagavad-gītā* (2.62) it is stated, *saṅgāt sañjāyate kāmaḥ:* one's desires and ambitions develop according to the company one keeps. It is often said that a man is known by his company, and if an ordinary man associates with devotees, he will certainly develop his dormant Kṛṣṇa consciousness. The understanding of Kṛṣṇa consciousness is innate in every living entity, and it is already developed to some extent when the living entity takes a human body. It is said in the *Caitanya-caritāmṛta* (*Madhya* 22.107):

> *nitya-siddha kṛṣṇa-prema 'sādhya' kabhu naya*
> *śravaṇādi-śuddha-citte karaye udaya*

"Pure love for Kṛṣṇa is eternally established in the hearts of living entities. It is not something to be gained from another source. When the heart is purified by hearing and chanting, this love naturally awakens." Since Kṛṣṇa consciousness is inherent in every living entity, everyone should be given a chance to hear about Kṛṣṇa. Simply by hearing and chanting—*śravaṇaṁ kīrtanam*—one's heart is directly purified, and one's original Kṛṣṇa consciousness is immediately awakened. Kṛṣṇa consciousness is not artificially imposed upon the heart; it is already there. When one chants the holy name of the Supreme Personality of Godhead, the heart is cleansed of all mundane contamination. In the first stanza of His *Śrī Śikṣāṣṭaka,* Lord Śrī Caitanya Mahāprabhu says:

ceto-darpaṇa-mārjanaṁ bhava-mahā-dāvāgni-
nirvāpaṇaṁ
śreyaḥ-kairava-candrikā-vitaraṇaṁ vidyā-vadhū-
jīvanam
ānandāmbudhi-vardhanaṁ prati-padaṁ
pūrṇāmṛtāsvādanaṁ
sarvātma-snapanaṁ paraṁ vijayate śrī-kṛṣṇa-
saṅkīrtanam

"All glories to the Śrī Kṛṣṇa *saṅkīrtana*, which cleanses the heart of all the dust accumulated for years and extinguishes the fire of conditional life, of repeated birth and death. This *saṅkīrtana* movement is the prime benediction for humanity at large because it spreads the rays of the benediction moon. It is the life of all transcendental knowledge. It increases the ocean of transcendental bliss, and it enables us to fully taste the nectar for which we are always anxious."

Not only is the chanter of the *mahā-mantra* purified, but the heart of anyone who happens to hear the transcendental vibration of Hare Kṛṣṇa, Hare Kṛṣṇa, Kṛṣṇa Kṛṣṇa, Hare Hare/ Hare Rāma, Hare Rāma, Rāma Rāma, Hare Hare is also cleansed. Even the souls embodied in lower animals, insects, trees and other species of life also become purified and prepared to become fully Kṛṣṇa conscious simply by hearing the transcendental vibration. This was explained by Ṭhākura Haridāsa when Caitanya Mahāprabhu inquired from him how living entities lower than human beings can be delivered from material bondage. Haridāsa Ṭhākura said that the chanting of the holy names is so powerful that even if one chants in the remotest parts of the jungle, the trees and animals will advance in Kṛṣṇa consciousness simply by hearing the vibration. This was actually proved by Śrī Caitanya Mahāprabhu Himself when He passed through the forest of Jhārikhaṇḍa. At that time the tigers, snakes, deer and all other animals abandoned their natural animosity and began chanting and dancing in *saṅkīrtana*. Of course, we cannot imitate the activities of Śrī Caitanya Mahāprabhu, but we should follow in His footsteps. We are not powerful enough to enchant the lower animals such as tigers, snakes, cats and dogs or entice them to dance, but by chanting the holy names of the Lord we can actually convert many people throughout the world to Kṛṣṇa consciousness. Contributing or distributing the holy name of the Lord is a sublime example of contributing or giving charity (the *dadāti* principle). By the same token, one must also follow the *pratigṛhṇāti* principle and be willing and ready to receive the transcendental gift. One should inquire about the Kṛṣṇa consciousness movement and open his mind in order to understand the situation of this material world. Thus the *guhyam ākhyāti pṛcchati* principles can be served.

The members of the International Society for Krishna Consciousness invite the Society's members and supporters to dine with them when they hold love feasts in all their branches every Sunday. Many interested people come to honor *prasādam,* and whenever possible they invite members of the Society to their homes and feed them sumptuously with *prasādam*. In this way both the members of the Society and the general public are benefited. People should give up the company of so-called *yogīs, jñānīs, karmīs* and philanthropists because their association can benefit no one. If one really wants to attain the goal of human life, he should associate with devotees of the Kṛṣṇa consciousness movement because it is the only movement that teaches one how to develop love of God. Religion is the special function of human society, and it constitutes the distinction between human society and animal society. Animal society has no church, mosque or religious system. In all parts of the world, however downtrodden human society may be, there is some system of religion. Even tribal aborigines in the jungles also have a system of religion. When a religious system develops and turns into love of God, it is successful. As stated in the First Canto of *Śrīmad-Bhāgavatam* (1.2.6):

sa vai puṁsāṁ paro dharmo
yato bhaktir adhokṣaje
ahaituky apratihatā
yayātmā suprasīdati

"The supreme occupation [*dharma*] for all humanity is that by which men can attain to loving devotional service unto the transcendent Lord. Such devotional service must be unmotivated and uninterrupted in order to completely satisfy the self."

If the members of human society actually want peace of mind, tranquillity and friendly relations between nations, they must follow the Kṛṣṇa conscious system of religion, by which they can develop their dormant love for Kṛṣṇa, the Supreme Personality of Godhead. As soon as people do so, their minds will immediately be filled with peace and tranquillity.

In this regard, Śrīla Bhaktisiddhānta Sarasvatī Ṭhākura warns all devotees engaged in broadcasting the Kṛṣṇa consciousness movement not to speak to the impersonalists, or Māyāvādīs, who are always determined to oppose such theistic movements. The world is full of Māyāvādīs and atheists, and the political parties of the world take advantage of Māyāvāda and other atheistic philosophies to promote materialism. Sometimes they even back a strong party to oppose the Kṛṣṇa consciousness movement. The Māyāvādīs and other atheists do not want the Kṛṣṇa consciousness movement to develop because it educates people in God consciousness. Such is the policy of the atheists. There is no benefit in feeding a snake milk and bananas because the snake will never be satisfied. On the contrary, by taking milk and bananas the snake simply becomes more poisonous (*kevalaṁ viṣa-vardhanam*). If a snake is given milk to drink, its poison simply increases. For a similar reason, we should not disclose our minds to the serpent Māyāvādīs and *karmīs*. Such disclosures will never help. It is best to completely avoid associating with them and never ask them about anything confidential because they cannot give good advice. Nor should we extend invitations to Māyāvādīs and atheists or accept their invitations, for by such intimate intermingling we may become affected by their atheistic mentality (*saṅgāt sañjāyate kāmaḥ*). It is the negative injunction of this verse that we should refrain from giving anything to or accepting anything from the Māyāvādīs and atheists. Śrī Caitanya Mahāprabhu has also warned, *viṣayīra anna khāile duṣṭa haya mana:* "When one eats food prepared by worldly people, one's mind becomes wicked." Unless one is very advanced, he is unable to utilize everyone's contribution to further the Kṛṣṇa consciousness movement; therefore on principle one should not accept charity from the Māyāvādīs or atheists. Indeed, Śrī Caitanya Mahāprabhu has forbidden devotees to associate even with ordinary men who are too addicted to material sense gratification.

The conclusion is that we should always keep company with devotees, observe the regulative devotional principles, follow in the footsteps of the *ācāryas* and in full obedience carry out the orders of the spiritual master. In this way we shall be able to develop our devotional service and dormant Kṛṣṇa consciousness. The devotee who is neither a neophyte nor a *mahā-bhāgavata* (a greatly advanced devotee) but is within the middle status of devotional service is expected to love the Supreme Personality of Godhead, make friends with the devotees, show favor to the ignorant and reject the jealous and demoniac. In this verse there is brief mention of the process of making loving transactions with the Supreme Personality of Godhead and making friends with the devotees. According to the *dadāti* principle, an advanced devotee is supposed to spend at least fifty percent of his income on the service of the Lord and His devotees. Śrīla Rūpa Gosvāmī has set such an example in his life. When he decided to retire, he distributed fifty percent of his life's earnings to Kṛṣṇa's service and twenty-five percent to his relatives and kept twenty-five percent for personal emergencies. This example should be followed by all devotees. Whatever one's income, fifty percent should be spent on behalf of Kṛṣṇa and His devotees, and this will fulfill the demands of *dadāti*.

In the next verse, Śrīla Rūpa Gosvāmī informs us what kind of Vaiṣṇava should be selected as a friend and how Vaiṣṇavas should be served.

TEXT FIVE

कृष्णेति यस्य गिरि तं मनसाद्रियेत
दीक्षास्ति चेत्प्रणतिभिश्च भजन्तमीशम् ।
शुश्रूषया भजनविज्ञमनन्यमन्य-
निन्दादिशून्यहृदमीप्सितसङ्गलब्ध्या ॥५॥

kṛṣṇeti yasya giri taṁ manasādriyeta
dīkṣāsti cet praṇatibhiś ca bhajantam īśam
śuśrūṣayā bhajana-vijñam ananyam anya-
nindādi-śūnya-hṛdam īpsita-saṅga-labdhyā

kṛṣṇa—the holy name of Lord Kṛṣṇa; *iti*—thus; *yasya*—of whom; *giri*—in the words or speech; *tam*—him; *manasā*—by the mind; *ādriyeta*—one must honor; *dīkṣā*—initiation; *asti*—there is; *cet*—if; *praṇatibhiḥ*—by obeisances; *ca*—also; *bhajantam*—engaged in devotional service; *īśam*—unto the Supreme Personality of Godhead; *śuśrūṣayā*—by practical service; *bhajana-vijñam*—one who is advanced in devotional service; *ananyam*—without deviation; *anya-nindā-ādi*—of blasphemy of others, etc.; *śūnya*—completely devoid; *hṛdam*—whose heart; *īpsita*—desirable; *saṅga*—association; *labdhyā*—by gaining.

TRANSLATION

One should mentally honor the devotee who chants the holy name of Lord Kṛṣṇa, one should offer humble obeisances to the devotee who has undergone spiritual initiation [dīkṣā] and is engaged in worshiping the

Deity, and one should associate with and faithfully serve that pure devotee who is advanced in undeviated devotional service and whose heart is completely devoid of the propensity to criticize others.

PURPORT

In order to intelligently apply the sixfold loving reciprocations mentioned in the previous verse, one must select proper persons with careful discrimination. Śrīla Rūpa Gosvāmī therefore advises that we should meet with the Vaiṣṇavas in an appropriate way, according to their particular status. In this verse he tells us how to deal with three types of devotees—the *kaniṣṭha-adhikārī*, *madhyama-adhikārī* and *uttama-adhikārī.* The *kaniṣṭha-adhikārī* is a neophyte who has received the *hari-nāma* initiation from the spiritual master and is trying to chant the holy name of Kṛṣṇa. One should respect such a person within his mind as a *kaniṣṭha-vaiṣṇava.* A *madhyama-adhikārī* has received spiritual initiation from the spiritual master and has been fully engaged by him in the transcendental loving service of the Lord. The *madhyama-adhikārī* should be considered to be situated midway in devotional service. The *uttama-adhikārī,* or highest devotee, is one who is very advanced in devotional service. An *uttama-adhikārī* is not interested in blaspheming others, his heart is completely clean, and he has attained the realized state of unalloyed Kṛṣṇa consciousness. According to Śrīla Rūpa Gosvāmī, the association and service of such a *mahā-bhāgavata,* or perfect Vaiṣṇava, are most desirable.

One should not remain a *kaniṣṭha-adhikārī,* one who is situated on the lowest platform of devotional service and is interested only in worshiping the Deity in the temple. Such a devotee is described in the Eleventh Canto of *Śrīmad-Bhāgavatam* (11.2.47):

arcāyām eva haraye
pūjāṁ yaḥ śraddhayehate
na tad-bhakteṣu cānyeṣu
sa bhaktaḥ prākṛtaḥ smṛtaḥ

"A person who is very faithfully engaged in the worship of the Deity in the temple, but who does not know how to behave toward devotees or people in general is called a *prākṛta-bhakta,* or *kaniṣṭha-adhikārī.*"

One therefore has to raise himself from the position of *kaniṣṭha-adhikārī* to the platform of *madhyama-adhikārī.* The *madhyama-adhikārī* is described in *Śrīmad-Bhāgavatam* (11.2.46) in this way:

īśvare tad-adhīneṣu
bāliśeṣu dviṣatsu ca
prema-maitrī-kṛpopekṣā
yaḥ karoti sa madhyamaḥ

"The *madhyama-adhikārī* is a devotee who worships the Supreme Personality of Godhead as the highest object of love, makes friends with the Lord's devotees, is merciful to the ignorant and avoids those who are envious by nature."

This is the way to cultivate devotional service properly;

therefore in this verse Śrīla Rūpa Gosvāmī has advised us how to treat various devotees. We can see from practical experience that there are different types of Vaiṣṇavas. The *prākṛta-sahajiyās* generally chant the Hare Kṛṣṇa *mahā-mantra,* yet they are attached to women, money and intoxication. Although such persons may chant the holy name of the Lord, they are not yet properly purified. Such people should be respected within one's mind, but their association should be avoided. Those who are innocent but simply carried away by bad association should be shown favor if they are eager to receive proper instructions from pure devotees, but those neophyte devotees who are actually initiated by the bona fide spiritual master and are seriously engaged in carrying out the orders of the spiritual master should be offered respectful obeisances.

In this Kṛṣṇa consciousness movement a chance is given to everyone without discrimination of caste, creed or color. Everyone is invited to join this movement, sit with us, take *prasādam* and hear about Kṛṣṇa. When we see that someone is actually interested in Kṛṣṇa consciousness and wants to be initiated, we accept him as a disciple for the chanting of the holy name of the Lord. When a neophyte devotee is actually initiated and engaged in devotional service by the orders of the spiritual master, he should be accepted immediately as a bona fide Vaiṣṇava, and obeisances should be offered unto him. Out of many such Vaiṣṇavas, one may be found to be very seriously engaged in the service of the Lord and strictly following all the regulative principles, chanting the prescribed number of rounds on *japa* beads and always thinking of how to expand the Kṛṣṇa consciousness movement. Such a Vaiṣṇava should be accepted as an *uttama-adhikārī,* a highly advanced devotee, and his association should always be sought.

The process by which a devotee becomes attached to Kṛṣṇa is described in the *Caitanya-caritāmṛta* (*Antya* 4.192):

dīkṣā-kāle bhakta kare ātma-samarpaṇa
sei-kāle kṛṣṇa tāre kare ātma-sama

"At the time of initiation, when a devotee fully surrenders to the service of the Lord, Kṛṣṇa accepts him to be as good as He Himself."

Dīkṣā, or spiritual initiation, is explained in the *Bhakti-sandarbha* (868) by Śrīla Jīva Gosvāmī:

divyaṁ jñānaṁ yato dadyāt
kuryāt pāpasya saṅkṣayam
tasmād dīkṣeti sā proktā
deśikais tattva-kovidaiḥ

"By *dīkṣā* one gradually becomes disinterested in material enjoyment and gradually becomes interested in spiritual life."

We have seen many practical examples of this, especially in Europe and America. Many students who come to us from rich and respectable families quickly lose all interest in material enjoyment and become very eager to enter into spiritual life. Although they come from very wealthy families, many of them accept living conditions that are not very comfortable. Indeed, for Kṛṣṇa's sake they are prepared to accept any living condition as long as they can live in the temple and associate with the Vaiṣṇavas. When one becomes so disinterested in material enjoyment, he becomes fit for initiation by the spiritual master. For the advancement of spiritual life *Śrīmad-Bhāgavatam* (6.1.13) prescribes: *tapasā brahmacaryeṇa śamena ca damena ca.* When a person is serious about accepting *dīkṣā,* he must be prepared to practice austerity, celibacy and control of the mind and body. If one is so prepared and is desirous of receiving spiritual enlightenment (*divyaṁ jñānam*), he is fit for being initiated. *Divyaṁ jñānam* is technically called *tad-vijñāna,* or knowledge about the Supreme. *Tad-vijñānārthaṁ sa gurum evābhigacchet:* when one is interested in the transcendental subject matter of the Absolute Truth, he should be initiated. Such a person should approach a spiritual master in order to take *dīkṣā.* *Śrīmad-Bhāgavatam* (11.3.21) also prescribes: *tasmād guruṁ prapadyeta jijñāsuḥ śreya uttamam.* "When one is actually interested in the transcendental science of the Absolute Truth, he should approach a spiritual master."

One should not accept a spiritual master without following his instructions. Nor should one accept a spiritual master just to make a fashionable show of spiritual life. One must be *jijñāsu,* very much inquisitive to learn from the bona fide spiritual master. The inquiries one makes should strictly pertain to transcendental science (*jijñāsuḥ śreya uttamam*). The word *uttamam* refers to that which is above material knowledge. *Tama* means "the darkness of this material world," and *ut* means "transcendental." Generally people are very interested in inquiring about mundane subject matters, but when one has lost such interest and is simply interested in transcendental subject matters, he is quite fit for being initiated. When one is actually initiated by the bona fide spiritual master and when he seriously engages in the service of the Lord, he should be accepted as a *madhyama-adhikārī*.

The chanting of the holy names of Kṛṣṇa is so sublime that if one chants the Hare Kṛṣṇa *mahā-mantra* offenselessly, carefully avoiding the ten offenses, he can certainly be gradually elevated to the point of understanding that there is no difference between the holy name of the Lord and the Lord Himself. One who has reached such an understanding should be very much respected by neophyte devotees. One should know for certain that without chanting the holy name of the Lord offenselessly, one cannot be a proper candidate for advancement in Kṛṣṇa consciousness. In *Śrī Caitanya-caritāmṛta* (*Madhya* 22.69) it is said:

yāhāra komala śraddhā, se 'kaniṣṭha' jana
krame krame teṅho bhakta ha-ibe 'uttama'

"One whose faith is soft and pliable is called a neophyte, but by gradually following the process, he will rise to the platform of a first-class devotee." Everyone begins his devotional life from the neophyte stage, but if one properly finishes chanting the prescribed number of rounds of *hari-nāma*, he is elevated step by step to the highest platform, *uttama-adhikārī*. The Kṛṣṇa consciousness movement prescribes sixteen rounds daily because people in the Western countries cannot concentrate for long periods while chanting on beads. Therefore the minimum number of rounds is prescribed. However, Śrīla Bhaktisiddhānta Sarasvatī Ṭhākura used to say that unless one chants at least sixty-four rounds of *japa* (one hundred thousand names), he is considered fallen (*patita*). According to his calculation, practically every one of us is fallen, but because we are trying to serve the Supreme Lord with all seriousness and without duplicity, we can expect the mercy of Lord Śrī Caitanya Mahāprabhu, who is famous as *patita-pāvana,* the deliverer of the fallen.

When Śrīla Satyarāja Khān, a great devotee of Śrī Caitanya Mahāprabhu, asked the Lord how a Vaiṣṇava could be recognized, the Lord replied:

prabhu kahe,—"yāṅra mukhe śuni eka-bāra
kṛṣṇa-nāma, sei pūjya,—śreṣṭha sabākāra"

"If one hears a person say the word 'Kṛṣṇa' even once, that person should be accepted as the best man out of the common group." (Cc. *Madhya* 15.106) Lord Caitanya Mahāprabhu continued:

"ataeva yāṅra mukhe eka kṛṣṇa-nāma
sei ta' vaiṣṇava, kariha tāṅhāra sammāna"

"One who is interested in chanting the holy name of Kṛṣṇa or who by practice likes to chant Kṛṣṇa's names should be accepted as a Vaiṣṇava and offered respects as such, at least within one's mind." (Cc. *Madhya* 15.111)

One of our friends, a famous English musician, has become attracted to chanting the holy names of Kṛṣṇa, and even in his records he has several times mentioned the holy name of Kṛṣṇa. At his home he offers respect to pictures of Kṛṣṇa and also to the preachers of Kṛṣṇa consciousness. In all regards, he has a very high estimation for Kṛṣṇa's name and Kṛṣṇa's activities; therefore we offer respects to him without reservation, for we are actually seeing that this gentleman is advancing gradually in Kṛṣṇa consciousness. Such a person should always be shown respect. The conclusion is that anyone who is trying to advance in Kṛṣṇa consciousness by regularly chanting the holy name should always be respected by Vaiṣṇavas. On the other hand, we have witnessed that some of our contemporaries who are supposed to be great preachers have gradually fallen into the material conception of life because they have failed to chant the holy name of the Lord.

While giving instructions to Sanātana Gosvāmī, Lord Caitanya Mahāprabhu divided devotional service into three categories.

śāstra-yukti nāhi jāne dṛḍha, śraddhāvān
'madhyama-adhikārī' sei mahā-bhāgyavān

"A person whose conclusive knowledge of the *śāstras* is not very strong but who has developed firm faith in chanting the Hare Kṛṣṇa *mahā-mantra* and who is also undeterred in the execution of his prescribed devotional service should be considered a *madhyama-adhikārī*. Such a person is very fortunate." (Cc. *Madhya* 22.67)

A *madhyama-adhikārī* is a *śraddhāvān,* a staunchly faithful person, and he is actually a candidate for further advancement in devotional service. Therefore in the *Caitanya-caritāmṛta* (*Madhya* 22.64) it is said:

śraddhāvān jana haya bhakti-adhikārī
'uttama', 'madhyama', 'kaniṣṭha'—śraddhā-anusārī

"One becomes qualified as a devotee on the elementary platform, the intermediate platform and the highest platform of devotional service according to the development of his *śraddhā* [faith]." Again in the *Caitanya-caritāmṛta* (*Madhya* 22.62) it is said:

'śraddhā'-śabde—viśvāsa kahe sudṛḍha niścaya
kṛṣṇe bhakti kaile sarva-karma kṛta haya

"*Śraddhā* is confident, firm faith that by rendering transcendental loving service to Kṛṣṇa one automatically performs all subsidiary activities. Such faith is favorable to the discharge of devotional service." *Śraddhā,* faith in Kṛṣṇa, is the beginning of Kṛṣṇa consciousness. Faith means strong faith. The words of the *Bhagavad-gītā* are authoritative instructions for faithful men, and whatever Kṛṣṇa says in the *Bhagavad-gītā* is to be accepted as it is, without interpretation. This was the way Arjuna accepted the *Bhagavad-gītā*. After hearing the *Bhagavad-gītā,* Arjuna told Kṛṣṇa: *sarvam etad ṛtaṁ manye yan māṁ vadasi keśava.* "O Kṛṣṇa, I totally accept as truth all that You have told me." (Bg. 10.14)

This is the correct way of understanding the *Bhagavad-gītā,* and this is called *śraddhā*. It is not that one accepts a portion of the *Bhagavad-gītā* according to his own whimsical interpretations and then rejects another portion. This is not *śraddhā*. *Śraddhā* means accepting the instructions of the *Bhagavad-gītā* in their totality, especially the last instruction: *sarva-dharmān parityajya mām ekaṁ śaraṇaṁ vraja*. "Abandon all varieties of religion and just surrender unto Me." (Bg. 18.66) When one becomes completely faithful in regard to this instruction, one's strong faith becomes the basis for advancing in spiritual life.

When one fully engages in chanting the Hare Kṛṣṇa *mahā-mantra,* he gradually realizes his own spiritual identity. Unless one faithfully chants the Hare Kṛṣṇa *mantra,* Kṛṣṇa does not reveal Himself: *sevonmukhe hi jihvādau svayam eva sphuraty adaḥ.* (*Bhakti-rasāmṛta-sindhu* 1.2.234) We cannot realize the Supreme Personality of Godhead by any artificial means. We must engage faithfully in the service of the Lord. Such service begins with the tongue (*sevonmukhe hi jihvādau*), which means that we should always chant the holy names of the Lord and accept *kṛṣṇa-prasādam.* We should not chant or accept anything else. When this process is faithfully followed, the Supreme Lord reveals Himself to the devotee.

When a person realizes himself to be an eternal servitor of Kṛṣṇa, he loses interest in everything but Kṛṣṇa's service. Always thinking of Kṛṣṇa, devising means by which to spread the holy name of Kṛṣṇa, he understands that his only business is in spreading the Kṛṣṇa consciousness movement all over the world. Such a person is to be recognized as an *uttama-adhikārī,* and his association should be immediately accepted according to the six processes (*dadāti pratigṛhṇāti,* etc.). Indeed, the advanced *uttama-adhikārī* Vaiṣṇava devotee should be accepted as a spiritual master. Everything one possesses should be offered to him, for it is enjoined that one should deliver whatever he has to the spiritual master. The *brahmacārī* in particular is supposed to beg alms from others and offer them to the spiritual master. However, one should not imitate the behavior of an advanced devotee or *mahā-bhāgavata* without being self-realized, for by such imitation one will eventually become degraded.

In this verse Śrīla Rūpa Gosvāmī advises the devotee to be intelligent enough to distinguish between the *kaniṣṭha-adhikārī, madhyama-adhikārī* and *uttama-adhikārī*. The devotee should also know his own position and should not try to imitate a devotee situated on a higher platform. Śrīla Bhaktivinoda Ṭhākura has given some practical hints to the effect that an *uttama-adhikārī* Vaiṣṇava can be recognized by his ability to convert many fallen souls to Vaiṣṇavism. One should not become a spiritual master unless he has attained the platform of *uttama-adhikārī*. A neophyte Vaiṣṇava or a Vaiṣṇava situated on the intermediate platform can also accept disciples, but such disciples must be on the same platform, and it should be understood that they cannot advance very well toward the ultimate goal of life under his insufficient guidance. Therefore a disciple should be careful to accept an *uttama-adhikārī* as a spiritual master.

TEXT SIX

दृष्टैः स्वभावजनितैर्वपुषश्च दोषैर्
न प्राकृतत्वमिह भक्त जनस्य पश्येत् ।

TEXT SIX

गङ्गाम्भसां न खलु बुद्बुदफेनपङ्कैर्
ब्रह्मद्रवत्वमपगच्छति नीरधर्मैः ॥६॥

dṛṣṭaiḥ svabhāva-janitair vapuṣaś ca doṣair
na prākṛtatvam iha bhakta-janasya paśyet
gaṅgāmbhasāṁ na khalu budbuda-phena-paṅkair
brahma-dravatvam apagacchati nīra-dharmaiḥ

dṛṣṭaiḥ—seen by ordinary vision; *svabhāva-janitaiḥ*—born of one's own nature; *vapuṣaḥ*—of the body; *ca*—and; *doṣaiḥ*—by the faults; *na*—not; *prākṛtatvam*—the state of being material; *iha*—in this world; *bhakta janasya*—of a pure devotee; *paśyet*—one should see; *gaṅgā-ambhasām*—of the Ganges waters; *na*—not; *khalu*—certainly; *budbuda-phena-paṅkaiḥ*—by bubbles, foam and mud; *brahma-dravatvam*—the transcendental nature; *apagacchati*—is spoiled; *nīra-dharmaiḥ*—the characteristics of water.

TRANSLATION

Being situated in his original Kṛṣṇa conscious position, a pure devotee does not identify with the body. Such a devotee should not be seen from a materialistic point of view. Indeed, one should overlook a devotee's having a body born in a low family, a body with a bad complexion, a deformed body, or a diseased or infirm body. According to ordinary vision, such imperfections may seem prominent in the body of a pure devotee, but despite such seeming defects, the body of a pure devotee cannot be polluted. It is exactly like the waters of the Ganges, which during the rainy season are sometimes full of bubbles, foam and

mud. The Ganges waters do not become polluted. Those who are advanced in spiritual understanding will bathe in the Ganges without considering the condition of the water.

PURPORT

Śuddha-bhakti, the activity of the soul proper—in other words, engagement in the transcendental loving service of the Lord—is performed in a liberated condition. In the *Bhagavad-gītā* (14.26) it is stated:

māṁ ca yo 'vyabhicāreṇa
bhakti-yogena sevate
sa guṇān samatītyaitān
brahma-bhūyāya kalpate

"One who engages in full devotional service, unfailing in all circumstances, at once transcends the modes of material nature and thus comes to the level of Brahman."

Avyabhicāriṇī bhakti means unalloyed devotion. A person engaged in devotional service must be free from material motives. In this Kṛṣṇa consciousness movement, one's consciousness must be changed. If consciousness is aimed toward material enjoyment, it is material consciousness, and if it is aimed toward serving Kṛṣṇa, it is Kṛṣṇa consciousness. A surrendered soul serves Kṛṣṇa without material considerations (*anyābhilāṣitā-śūnyam.*) *Jñāna-karmādy-anāvṛtam:* unalloyed devotional service, which is transcendental to such activities of the mind and body as *jñāna* (mental speculation) and *karma* (fruitive work), is called pure *bhakti-yoga. Bhakti-yoga* is the proper activity of the soul, and when one actually engages in unalloyed, uncontaminated devotional service, he is already liberated (*sa guṇān samatītyaitān*). Kṛṣṇa's devotee is not subjected to material conditions, even though his bodily features may appear materially conditioned. One should therefore not see a pure devotee from a materialistic point of view. Unless one is actually a devotee, he cannot see another devotee perfectly. As explained in the previous verse, there are three types of devotees—*kaniṣṭha-adhikārī*, *madhyama-adhikārī* and *uttama-adhikārī*. The *kaniṣṭha-adhikārī* cannot distinguish between a devotee and nondevotee. He is simply concerned with worshiping the Deity in the temple. A *madhyama-adhikārī*, however, can distinguish between the devotee and nondevotee, as well as between the devotee and the Lord. Thus he treats the Supreme Personality of Godhead, the devotee and the nondevotee in different ways.

No one should criticize the bodily defects of a pure devotee. If there are such defects, they should be overlooked. What should be taken into account is the spiritual master's main business, which is devotional service, pure service to the Supreme Lord. As stated in the *Bhagavad-gītā* (9.30):

api cet sudurācāro
bhajate mām ananya-bhāk
sādhur eva sa mantavyaḥ
samyag vyavasito hi saḥ

Even if a devotee sometimes seems to engage in abominable activities, he should be considered a *sādhu*, a saintly person, because his actual identity is that of one engaged in the loving service of the Lord. In other words, he is not to be considered an ordinary human being.

Even though a pure devotee may not be born in a *brāhmaṇa* or *gosvāmī* family, if he is engaged in the service of the Lord he should not be neglected. In actuality there cannot be a family of *gosvāmīs* based on material considerations, caste or heredity. The *gosvāmī* title is actually the monopoly of the pure devotees; thus we speak of the Six Gosvāmīs, headed by Rūpa Gosvāmī and Sanātana Gosvāmī. Rūpa Gosvāmī and Sanātana Gosvāmī had practically become Mohammedans and had therefore changed their names to Dabira Khāsa and Sākara Mallika, but Śrī Caitanya Mahāprabhu Himself made them *gosvāmīs*. Therefore the *gosvāmī* title is not hereditary. The word *gosvāmī* refers to one who can control his senses, who is master of the senses. A devotee is not controlled by the senses, but is the controller of the senses. Consequently he should be called *svāmī* or *gosvāmī*, even though he may not be born in a *gosvāmī* family.

According to this formula, the *gosvāmīs* who are descendants of Śrī Nityānanda Prabhu and Śrī Advaita Prabhu are certainly devotees, but devotees coming from other families should not be discriminated against; indeed, whether the devotees come from a family of previous *ācāryas* or from an ordinary family, they should be treated equally. One should not think, "Oh, here is an American *gosvāmī*," and discriminate against him. Nor should one think, "Here is a *nityānanda-vaṁśa-gosvāmī*." There is an undercurrent of protest against our awarding the title *gosvāmī* to the American

Vaiṣṇavas of the Kṛṣṇa consciousness movement. Sometimes people flatly tell the American devotees that their *sannyāsa* or title of *gosvāmī* is not bona fide. However, according to the statements of Śrīla Rūpa Gosvāmī in this verse, an American *gosvāmī* and a *gosvāmī* in a family of *ācāryas* are nondifferent.

On the other hand, a devotee who has attained the title of *gosvāmī* but is not born of a *brāhmaṇa* father or of a *gosvāmī* in the family of Nityānanda or Advaita Prabhu should not be artificially puffed up by thinking that he has become a *gosvāmī*. He should always remember that as soon as he becomes materially puffed up, he immediately falls down. This Kṛṣṇa consciousness movement is a transcendental science, and there is no room for jealousy. This movement is meant for the *paramahaṁsas* who are completely free from all jealousy (*paramaṁ nirmatsarāṇām*). One should not be jealous, whether he is born in a family of *gosvāmīs* or has the title of *gosvāmī* awarded to him. As soon as anyone becomes envious, he falls from the platform of *paramahaṁsa*.

If we consider the bodily defects of a Vaiṣṇava, we should understand that we are committing an offense at the lotus feet of the Vaiṣṇava. An offense at the lotus feet of a Vaiṣṇava is very serious. Indeed, Śrī Caitanya Mahāprabhu has described this offense as *hātī-mātā,* the mad elephant offense. A mad elephant can create a disaster, especially when it enters into a nicely trimmed garden. One should therefore be very careful not to commit any offense against a Vaiṣṇava. Every devotee should be ready to take instructions from a superior Vaiṣṇava, and a superior Vaiṣṇava must be ready to help an inferior Vaiṣṇava in all respects. One is superior or inferior according to his spiritual development in Kṛṣṇa consciousness. One is forbidden to observe the activities of a pure Vaiṣṇava from a material point of view. For the neophyte especially, considering a pure devotee from a material point of view is very injurious. One should therefore avoid observing a pure devotee externally, but should try to see the internal features and understand how he is engaged in the transcendental loving service of the Lord. In this way one can avoid seeing the pure devotee from a material point of view, and thus one can gradually become a purified devotee himself.

Those who think that Kṛṣṇa consciousness is limited to a certain section of people, a certain section of devotees or a certain tract of land are generally prone to see the external features of a devotee. Such neophytes, unable to appreciate the exalted service of the advanced devotee, try to bring the *mahā-bhāgavata* to their platform. We experience such difficulty in propagating Kṛṣṇa consciousness all over the world. Unfortunately we are surrounded by neophyte Godbrothers who do not appreciate the extraordinary activities of spreading Kṛṣṇa consciousness all over the world. They simply try to bring us to their platform, and they try to criticize us in every respect. We very much regret their naive activities and poor fund of knowledge. An empowered person who is actually engaged in the confidential service of the Lord should not be treated as an ordinary human being, for it is stated that unless one is empowered by Kṛṣṇa, one cannot spread the Kṛṣṇa consciousness movement all over the world.

When one thus criticizes a pure devotee, he commits an offense (*vaiṣṇava-aparādha*) that is very obstructive and dangerous for those who desire to advance in Kṛṣṇa consciousness. A person cannot derive any spiritual benefit when he offends the lotus feet of a Vaiṣṇava. Everyone should therefore be very careful not to be jealous of an empowered Vaiṣṇava, or a *śuddha-vaiṣṇava*. It is also an offense to consider an empowered Vaiṣṇava an object of disciplinary action. It is offensive to try to give him advice or to correct him. One can distinguish between a neophyte Vaiṣṇava and an advanced Vaiṣṇava by their activities. The advanced Vaiṣṇava is always situated as the spiritual master, and the neophyte is always considered his disciple. The spiritual master must not be subjected to the advice of a disciple, nor should a spiritual master be obliged to take instructions from those who are not his disciples. This is the sum and substance of Śrīla Rūpa Gosvāmī's advice in the sixth verse.

TEXT SEVEN

स्यात्कृष्णनामचरितादिसिताप्यविद्या-
पित्तोपतप्तरसनस्य न रोचिका नु ।
किन्त्वादरादनुदिनं खलु सैव जुष्टा
स्वाद्वी क्रमाद्भवति तद्गदमूलहन्त्री ॥७॥

syāt kṛṣṇa-nāma-caritādi-sitāpy avidyā-
pittopatapta-rasanasya na rocikā nu

kintv ādarād anudinaṁ khalu saiva juṣṭā
svādvī kramād bhavati tad-gada-mūla-hantrī

syāt—is; *kṛṣṇa*—of Lord Kṛṣṇa; *nāma*—the holy name; *carita-ādi*—the character, pastimes and so forth; *sitā*—sugar candy; *api*—although; *avidyā*—of ignorance; *pitta*—by the bile; *upatapta*—afflicted; *rasanasya*—of the tongue; *na*—not; *rocikā*—palatable; *nu*—oh, how wonderful it is; *kintu*—but; *ādarāt*—carefully; *anudinam*—every day, or twenty-four hours daily; *khalu*—naturally; *sā*—that (sugar candy of the holy name, character, pastimes and so forth); *eva*—certainly; *juṣṭā*—taken or chanted; *svādvī*—relishable; *kramāt*—gradually; *bhavati*—becomes; *tat-gada*—of that disease; *mūla*—of the root; *hantrī*—the destroyer.

TRANSLATION

The holy name, character, pastimes and activities of Kṛṣṇa are all transcendentally sweet like sugar candy. Although the tongue of one afflicted by the jaundice of avidyā [ignorance] cannot taste anything sweet, it is wonderful that simply by carefully chanting these sweet names every day, a natural relish awakens within his tongue, and his disease is gradually destroyed at the root.

PURPORT

Lord Kṛṣṇa's holy name, qualities, pastimes and so forth are all of the nature of absolute truth, beauty and bliss.

Naturally they are very sweet, like sugar candy, which appeals to everyone. Nescience, however, is compared to the disease called jaundice, which is caused by bilious secretions. Attacked by jaundice, the tongue of a diseased person cannot palatably relish sugar candy. Rather, a person with jaundice considers something sweet to taste very bitter. *Avidyā* (ignorance) similarly perverts the ability to relish the transcendentally palatable name, qualities, form and pastimes of Kṛṣṇa. Despite this disease, if one with great care and attention takes to Kṛṣṇa consciousness, chanting the holy name and hearing Kṛṣṇa's transcendental pastimes, his ignorance will be destroyed and his tongue enabled to taste the sweetness of the transcendental nature of Kṛṣṇa and His paraphernalia. Such a recovery of spiritual health is possible only by the regular cultivation of Kṛṣṇa consciousness.

When a man in the material world takes more interest in the materialistic way of life than in Kṛṣṇa consciousness, he is considered to be in a diseased condition. The normal condition is to remain an eternal servant of the Lord (*jīvera 'svarūpa' haya—kṛṣṇera 'nitya-dāsa'*). This healthy condition is lost when the living entity forgets Kṛṣṇa due to being attracted by the external features of Kṛṣṇa's *māyā* energy. This world of *māyā* is called *durāśraya,* which means "false or bad shelter." One who puts his faith in *durāśraya* becomes a candidate for hoping against hope. In the material world everyone is trying to become happy, and although their material attempts are baffled in every way, due to their nescience they cannot understand their mistakes. People try to rectify one mistake by making another mistake. This is the way of the struggle for existence in the material world. If one in this condition is advised to take to Kṛṣṇa consciousness and be happy, he does not accept such instructions.

This Kṛṣṇa consciousness movement is being spread all over the world just to remedy this gross ignorance. People in general are misled by blind leaders. The leaders of human society—the politicians, philosophers and scientists—are blind because they are not Kṛṣṇa conscious. According to the *Bhagavad-gītā* (7.15), because they are bereft of all factual knowledge due to their atheistic way of life, they are actually sinful rascals and are the lowest among men:

na māṁ duṣkṛtino mūḍhāḥ
prapadyante narādhamāḥ
māyayāpahṛta jñānā-
āsuraṁ bhāvam āśritāḥ

"Those miscreants who are grossly foolish, who are lowest among mankind, whose knowledge is stolen by illusion, and who partake of the atheistic nature of demons do not surrender unto Me."

Such people never surrender to Kṛṣṇa, and they oppose the endeavor of those who wish to take Kṛṣṇa's shelter. When such atheists become leaders of society, the entire atmosphere is surcharged with nescience. In such a condition, people do not become very enthusiastic to receive this Kṛṣṇa consciousness movement, just as a diseased person suffering from jaundice does not relish the taste of sugar candy. However, one must know that for jaundice, sugar candy is the only specific medicine. Similarly, in the present confused state of humanity, Kṛṣṇa consciousness, the chanting of the holy name of the Lord—Hare Kṛṣṇa, Hare Kṛṣṇa, Kṛṣṇa Kṛṣṇa, Hare Hare/ Hare Rāma, Hare Rāma, Rāma Rāma, Hare Hare—is the only remedy for setting the world aright. Although Kṛṣṇa consciousness may not be very palatable for a diseased person, Śrīla Rūpa Gosvāmī nonetheless advises that if one wants to be cured of the material disease, he must take to it with great care and attention. One begins his treatment by chanting the Hare Kṛṣṇa *mahā-mantra* because by chanting this holy name of the Lord a person in the material condition will be relieved from all misconceptions (*ceto-darpaṇa-mārjanam*). *Avidyā,* a misconception about one's spiritual identity, provides the foundation for *ahaṅkāra,* or false ego within the heart.

The real disease is in the heart. If the mind is cleansed, however, if consciousness is cleansed, a person cannot be harmed by the material disease. To cleanse the mind and heart from all misconceptions, one should take to this chanting of the Hare Kṛṣṇa *mahā-mantra.* This is both easy and beneficial. By chanting the holy name of the Lord, one is immediately freed from the blazing fire of material existence.

There are three stages in chanting the holy name of the Lord—the offensive stage, the stage of lessening offenses, and the pure stage. When a neophyte takes to the chanting of the Hare Kṛṣṇa *mantra,* he generally commits many offenses. There are ten basic offenses, and if the devotee avoids these, he can glimpse the next stage, which is situated between offensive chanting and pure chanting. When one attains the pure stage, he is immediately liberated. This is called *bhava-mahā-dāvāgni-nirvāpanam.* As soon as one is liberated from the blazing fire of material existence, he can relish the taste of transcendental life.

The conclusion is that in order to get freed from the material disease, one must take to the chanting of the Hare Kṛṣṇa *mantra.* The Kṛṣṇa consciousness movement is especially meant for creating an atmosphere in which people can take to the chanting of the Hare Kṛṣṇa *mantra.* One must begin with faith, and when this faith is increased by chanting, a person can become a member of the Society. We are sending *saṅkīrtana* parties all over the world, and they are experiencing that even in the remotest part of the world, where there is no knowledge of Kṛṣṇa, the Hare Kṛṣṇa *mahā-mantra* attracts thousands of men to our camp. In some areas, people begin to imitate the devotees by shaving their heads and chanting the Hare Kṛṣṇa *mahā-mantra,* only a few days after hearing the *mantra.* This may be imitative, but imitation of a good thing is desired. Some imitators gradually become interested in being initiated by the spiritual master and offer themselves for initiation.

If one is sincere, he is initiated, and this stage is called *bhajana-kriyā.* One then actually engages in the service of the Lord by regularly chanting the Hare Kṛṣṇa *mahā-mantra,* sixteen rounds daily, and refraining from illicit sex, intoxicants, meat-eating and gambling. By *bhajana-kriyā* one attains freedom from the contamination of materialistic life. He no longer goes to a restaurant or hotel to taste so-called palatable dishes made with meat and onions, nor does he care to smoke or drink tea or coffee. He not only refrains from illicit sex, but avoids sex life entirely. Nor is he interested in wasting his time

His Divine Grace
A. C. Bhaktivedanta Swami Prabhupāda
Founder-*Ācārya*
of the International Society for Krishna Consciousness

Śrīla Rūpa Gosvāmī, the author of *Śrī Upadeśāmṛta* and numerous other volumes of Vaiṣṇava philosophy. He is the chief disciple of Śrī Kṛṣṇa Caitanya, the pioneer of the powerful *saṅkīrtana* movement that began in India five hundred years ago.

Lord Caitanya Mahāprabhu and His intimate associates performing *saṅkīrtana* (congregational chanting of the holy names of God). In the front row, from left to right, are Śrī Advaita Ācārya, Lord Nityānanda, Lord Caitanya, Śrī Gadādhara, and Śrī Śrīvāsa.

Śrī Śrī Rādhā-Kṛṣṇa, the Supreme Personality of Godhead and His eternal consort. Of the many objects of favored delight and of all the beloved damsels in Vṛndāvana, Śrīmatī Rādhārāṇī is the most treasured object of Kṛṣṇa's love. (p. 82)

The temple of Rādhā-Govinda in Vṛndāvana, India, established in the sixteenth century by Śrīla Rūpa Gosvāmī. A conquering Moghul tyrant, Aurangzeb, dismantled the top four stories in envy of the temple's magnificence.

Śrī Śrī Rādhā-Govindajī, the beloved Deities of Śrīla Rūpa Gosvāmī. At the time of the Moghul invasion, they were moved to Jaipur, India, where they are presently being worshiped.

Lord Kṛṣṇa lifting Govardhana Hill during His pastimes in Vṛndāvana, India, five thousand years ago. Kṛṣṇa held up the divine hill for seven days to protect the denizens of Vṛndāvana from torrential rains sent by Indra, the king of the demigods. (p. 79)

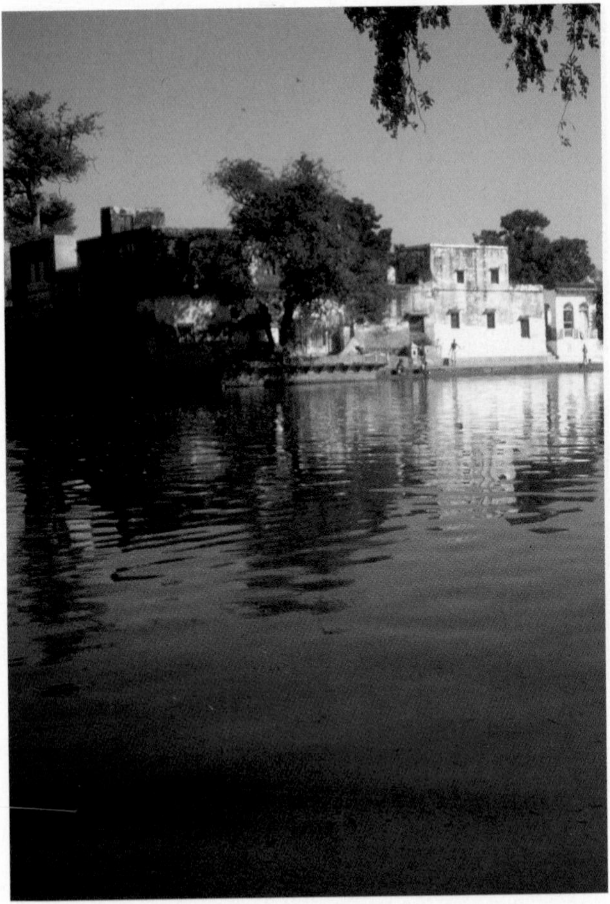

Śrī Rādhā-kuṇḍa, located in the district of Mathurā, India, is exalted because it belongs to Śrīmatī Rādhārāṇī, who is the most beloved object of Śrī Kṛṣṇa. Among all the *gopīs,* She is the most beloved. Similarly, Her lake, Śrī Rādhā-kuṇḍa, is as dear to Kṛṣṇa as Rādhā Herself. (p. 90)

in speculating or gambling. In this way it is to be understood that one is becoming cleansed of unwanted things (*anartha-nivṛtti*). The word *anartha* refers to unwanted things. *Anarthas* are vanquished when one becomes attached to the Kṛṣṇa consciousness movement.

When a person is relieved from unwanted things, he becomes fixed in executing his Kṛṣṇa activities. Indeed, he becomes attached to such activities and experiences ecstasy in executing devotional service. This is called *bhāva,* the preliminary awakening of dormant love of Godhead. Thus the conditioned soul becomes free from material existence and loses interest in the bodily conception of life, including material opulence, material knowledge and material attraction of all variety. At such a time one can understand who the Supreme Personality of Godhead is and what His *māyā* is.

Although *māyā* may be present, it cannot disturb a devotee once he attains the *bhāva* stage. This is because the devotee can see the real position of *māyā. Māyā* means forgetfulness of Kṛṣṇa, and forgetfulness of Kṛṣṇa and Kṛṣṇa consciousness stand side by side like shadow and light. If one remains in shadow, he cannot enjoy the facilities offered by light, and if one remains in light, he cannot be disturbed by the darkness of shadow. By taking to Kṛṣṇa consciousness, one gradually becomes liberated and remains in the light. Indeed, he does not even touch the darkness. As confirmed in *Caitanya-caritāmṛta* (*Madhya* 22.31):

> *kṛṣṇa—sūrya-sama; māyā haya andhakāra*
> *yāhāṅ kṛṣṇa, tāhāṅ nāhi māyāra adhikāra*

"Kṛṣṇa is compared to sunshine, and *māyā* is compared to darkness. Wherever there is sunshine, there cannot be darkness. As soon as one takes to Kṛṣṇa consciousness, the darkness of illusion, the influence of the external energy, will immediately vanish."

TEXT EIGHT

तन्नामरूपचरितादिसुकीर्तनानु-
स्मृत्योः क्रमेण रसनामनसी नियोज्य ।
तिष्ठन् व्रजे तदनुरागि जनानुगामी
कालं नयेदखिलमित्युपदेशसारम् ॥८॥

tan-nāma-rūpa-caritādi-sukīrtanānu-
smṛtyoḥ krameṇa rasanā-manasī niyojya
tiṣṭhan vraje tad-anurāgi janānugāmī
kālaṁ nayed akhilam ity upadeśa-sāram

tat—of Lord Kṛṣṇa; *nāma*—the holy name; *rūpa*—form; *carita-ādi*—character, pastimes and so on; *su-kīrtana*—in discussing or chanting nicely; *anu-smṛtyoḥ*—and in remembering; *krameṇa*—gradually; *rasanā*—the tongue; *manasī*—and one's mind; *ni-yojya*—engaging; *tiṣṭhan*—residing; *vraje*—in Vraja; *tat*—to Lord Kṛṣṇa; *anurāgi*—attached; *jana*—persons; *anugāmī*—following; *kālam*—time; *nayet*—should utilize; *akhilam*—full; *iti*—thus; *upadeśa*—of advice or instruction; *sāram*—the essence.

TRANSLATION

The essence of all advice is that one should utilize one's full time—twenty-four hours a day—in nicely chanting and remembering the Lord's divine name, transcendental form, qualities and eternal pastimes, thereby gradually engaging one's tongue and mind. In this way one should reside in Vraja [Goloka Vṛndāvana-dhāma] and serve Kṛṣṇa under the guidance of devotees. One should follow in the footsteps of the Lord's beloved devotees, who are deeply attached to His devotional service.

PURPORT

Since the mind may be one's enemy or one's friend, one has to train the mind to become his friend. The Kṛṣṇa consciousness movement is especially meant for training the mind to be always engaged in Kṛṣṇa's business. The mind contains hundreds and thousands of impressions, not only of this life but also of many, many lives of the past. These impressions sometimes come in contact with one another and produce contradictory pictures. In this way the mind's function can become dangerous for a conditioned soul. Students of psychology are aware of the mind's various psychological changes. In the *Bhagavad-gītā* (8.6) it is said:

yaṁ yaṁ vāpi smaran bhāvaṁ
tyajaty ante kalevaram
taṁ tam evaiti kaunteya
sadā tad-bhāva-bhāvitaḥ

"Whatever state of being one remembers when he quits his body, that state he will attain without fail."

At the time of death, the mind and intelligence of a living entity create the subtle form of a certain type of body for the next life. If the mind suddenly thinks of something not very congenial, one has to take a corresponding birth in the next life. On the other hand, if one can think of Kṛṣṇa at the time of death, he can be transferred to the spiritual world, Goloka Vṛndāvana. This process of transmigration is very subtle; therefore Śrīla Rūpa Gosvāmī advises devotees to train their minds in order that they will be unable to remember anything other than Kṛṣṇa. Similarly, the tongue should be trained to speak only of Kṛṣṇa and to taste only *kṛṣṇa-prasādam*. Śrīla Rūpa Gosvāmī further advises, *tiṣṭhan vraje:* one should live in Vṛndāvana or any part of Vrajabhūmi. Vrajabhūmi, or the land of Vṛndāvana, is supposed to be eighty-four *krośas* in area. One *krośa* equals two square miles. When one makes Vṛndāvana his residence, he should take shelter of an advanced devotee there. In this way one should always think of Kṛṣṇa and His pastimes. This is further elucidated by Śrīla Rūpa Gosvāmī in his *Bhakti-rasāmṛta-sindhu* (1.2.294):

kṛṣṇaṁ smaran janaṁ cāsya
preṣṭhaṁ nija-samīhitam
tat-tat-kathā-rataś cāsau
kuryād vāsaṁ vraje sadā

"A devotee should always reside in the transcendental realm of Vraja and always engage in *kṛṣṇaṁ smaran janaṁ cāsya preṣṭham*, the remembrance of Śrī Kṛṣṇa and His beloved associates. By following in the footsteps of such associates and by entering under their eternal guidance, one can acquire an intense desire to serve the Supreme Personality of Godhead."

Again, Śrīla Rūpa Gosvāmī states in *Bhakti-rasāmṛta-sindhu* (1.2.295):

sevā sādhaka-rūpeṇa
siddha-rūpeṇa cātra hi
tad-bhāva-lipsunā kāryā
vraja-lokānusārataḥ

"In the transcendental realm of Vraja [Vraja-dhāma] one should serve the Supreme Lord, Śrī Kṛṣṇa, with a feeling similar to that of His associates, and one should place himself under the direct guidance of a particular associate of Kṛṣṇa and should follow in his footsteps. This method is applicable both in the stage of *sādhana* [spiritual practices executed while in the stage of bondage] and in the stage of *sādhya* [God realization], when one is a *siddha-puruṣa*, or a spiritually perfect soul."

Śrīla Bhaktisiddhānta Sarasvatī Ṭhākura has commented as follows upon this verse: "One who has not yet developed interest in Kṛṣṇa consciousness should give up all material motives and train his mind by following the progressive regulative principles, namely chanting and remembering Kṛṣṇa and His name, form, qualities, pastimes and so forth. In this way, after developing a taste for such things, one should try to live in Vṛndāvana and pass his time constantly remembering

Kṛṣṇa's name, fame, pastimes and qualities under the direction and protection of an expert devotee. This is the sum and substance of all instruction regarding the cultivation of devotional service.

"In the neophyte stage one should always engage in hearing *kṛṣṇa-kathā.* This is called *śravaṇa-daśā,* the stage of hearing. By constantly hearing the transcendental holy name of Kṛṣṇa and hearing of His transcendental form, qualities and pastimes, one can attain to the stage of acceptance, called *varaṇa-daśā.* When one attains this stage, he becomes attached to the hearing of *kṛṣṇa-kathā.* When one is able to chant in ecstasy, he attains the stage of *smaraṇāvasthā,* the stage of remembering. Recollection, absorption, meditation, constant remembrance and trance are the five items of progressive *kṛṣṇa-smaraṇa.* At first, remembrance of Kṛṣṇa may be interrupted at intervals, but later remembrance proceeds uninterrupted. When remembrance is uninterrupted, it becomes concentrated and is called meditation. When meditation expands and becomes constant, it is called *anusmṛti.* By uninterrupted and unceasing *anusmṛti* one enters the stage of *samādhi,* or spiritual trance. After *smaraṇa-daśā* or *samādhi* has fully developed, the soul comes to understand his original constitutional position. At that time he can perfectly and clearly understand his eternal relationship with Kṛṣṇa. That is called *sampatti-daśā,* the perfection of life.

"The *Caitanya-caritāmṛta* advises those who are neophytes to give up all kinds of motivated desires and simply engage in the regulative devotional service of the Lord according to the directions of scripture. In this way a neophyte can gradually develop attachment for

Kṛṣṇa's name, fame, form, qualities and so forth. When one has developed such attachment, he can spontaneously serve the lotus feet of Kṛṣṇa even without following the regulative principles. This stage is called *rāga-bhakti,* or devotional service in spontaneous love. At that stage the devotee can follow in the footsteps of one of the eternal associates of Kṛṣṇa in Vṛndāvana. This is called *rāgānuga-bhakti. Rāgānuga-bhakti,* or spontaneous devotional service, can be executed in *śānta-rasa* when one aspires to be like Kṛṣṇa's cows or the stick or flute in Kṛṣṇa's hand or the flowers around Kṛṣṇa's neck. In *dāsya-rasa* one follows in the footsteps of servants like Citraka, Patraka or Raktaka. In friendship, *sakhya-rasa,* one can become a friend like Baladeva, Śrīdāmā or Sudāmā. In *vātsalya-rasa,* characterized by parental affection, one can become like Nanda Mahārāja or Yaśodā, and in *mādhurya-rasa,* characterized by conjugal love, one can become like Śrīmatī Rādhārāṇī or Her lady friends such as Lalitā or Her serving maids (*mañjarīs*) like Rūpa and Rati. This is the essence of all instruction in the matter of devotional service."

TEXT NINE

वैकुण्ठाज्जनितो वरा मधुपुरी तत्रापि रासोत्सवाद्
वृन्दारण्यमुदारपाणिरमणात्तत्रापि गोवर्धनः ।
राधाकुण्डमिहापि गोकुलपतेः प्रेमामृताप्लावनात्
कुर्यादस्य विराजतो गिरितटे सेवां विवेकी न कः ॥९॥

vaikuṇṭhāj janito varā madhu-purī tatrāpi rāsotsavād
vṛndāraṇyam udāra-pāṇi-ramaṇāt tatrāpi govardhanaḥ
rādhā-kuṇḍam ihāpi gokula-pateḥ premāmṛtāplāvanāt
kuryād asya virājato giri-taṭe sevāṁ vivekī na kaḥ

vaikuṇṭhāt—than Vaikuṇṭha, the spiritual world; *janitaḥ*—because of birth; *varā*—better; *madhu-purī*—the transcendental city known as Mathurā; *tatra api*—superior to that; *rāsa-utsavāt*—because of the performance of the *rāsa-līlā; vṛndā-araṇyam*—the forest of Vṛndāvana; *udāra-pāṇi*—of Lord Kṛṣṇa; *ramaṇāt*—because of various kinds of loving pastimes; *tatra api*—superior to that; *govardhanaḥ*—Govardhana Hill; *rādhā-kuṇḍam*—a place called Rādhā-kuṇḍa; *iha api*—superior to this; *gokula-pateḥ*—of Kṛṣṇa, the master of Gokula; *prema-amṛta*—with the nectar of divine love; *āplāvanāt*—because of being overflooded; *kuryāt*—would do; *asya*—of this (Rādhā-kuṇḍa); *virājataḥ*—situated; *giri-taṭe*—at the foot of Govardhana Hill; *sevām*—service; *vivekī*—who is intelligent; *na*—not; *kaḥ*—who.

TRANSLATION

The holy place known as Mathurā is spiritually superior to Vaikuṇṭha, the transcendental world, because the Lord appeared there. Superior to Mathurā-purī is the transcendental forest of Vṛndāvana because of Kṛṣṇa's rāsa-līlā pastimes. And superior to the forest

of Vṛndāvana is Govardhana Hill, for it was raised by the divine hand of Śrī Kṛṣṇa and was the site of His various loving pastimes. And, above all, the superexcellent Śrī Rādhā-kuṇḍa stands supreme, for it is overflooded with the ambrosial nectarean prema of the Lord of Gokula, Śrī Kṛṣṇa. Where, then, is that intelligent person who is unwilling to serve this divine Rādhā-kuṇḍa, which is situated at the foot of Govardhana Hill?

PURPORT

The spiritual world is three fourths of the total creation of the Supreme Personality of Godhead, and it is the most exalted region. The spiritual world is naturally superior to the material world; however, Mathurā and the adjoining areas, although appearing in the material world, are considered superior to the spiritual world because the Supreme Personality of Godhead Himself appeared at Mathurā. The interior forests of Vṛndāvana are considered superior to Mathurā because of the presence of the twelve forests (*dvādaśa-vana*), such as Tālavana, Madhuvana and Bahulāvana, which are famous for the various pastimes of the Lord. But superior to these forests is the divine Govardhana Hill because Kṛṣṇa lifted it like an umbrella, raising it with His beautiful lotuslike hand to protect His associates, the denizens of Vraja, from the torrential rains sent by angry Indra, King of the demigods. It is also at Govardhana Hill that Kṛṣṇa tended the cows with His cowherd friends, and there also He had His rendezvous with His most beloved Śrī Rādhā and engaged in loving pastimes with Her. Rādhā-kuṇḍa, at the foot of Govardhana, is superior to all because it is there that love of Kṛṣṇa overflows. Advanced devotees prefer to reside at Rādhā-kuṇḍa because this place is the site of many memories of the eternal loving affairs between Kṛṣṇa and Rādhārāṇī (*rati-vilāsa*).

In the *Caitanya-caritāmṛta* (*Madhya-līlā,* Chapter Eighteen) it is stated that when Śrī Caitanya Mahāprabhu first visited the area of Vrajabhūmi, He could not at first find the location of Rādhā-kuṇḍa. This means that Śrī Caitanya Mahāprabhu was actually searching for the exact location of Rādhā-kuṇḍa. Finally He found the holy spot, and there was a small pond there. He took His bath in that small pond and told His devotees that the actual Rādhā-kuṇḍa was situated there. Later the pond was excavated by Lord Caitanya's devotees, headed first by the Six Gosvāmīs, such as Rūpa and Raghunātha Dāsa. Presently there is a large lake known as Rādhā-kuṇḍa there. Śrīla Rūpa Gosvāmī has given much stress to Rādhā-kuṇḍa because of Śrī Caitanya Mahāprabhu's desire to find it. Who, then, would give up Rādhā-kuṇḍa and try to reside elsewhere? No person with transcendental intelligence would do so. The importance of Rādhā-kuṇḍa, however, cannot be realized by other Vaiṣṇava *sampradāyas,* nor can persons uninterested in the devotional service of Lord Caitanya Mahāprabhu understand the spiritual importance and divine nature of Rādhā-kuṇḍa. Thus Rādhā-kuṇḍa is mainly worshiped by the Gauḍīya Vaiṣṇavas, the followers of Lord Śrī Kṛṣṇa Caitanya Mahāprabhu.

TEXT TEN

कर्मिभ्यः परितो हरेः प्रियतया व्यक्तिं ययुर्ज्ञानिनस्
तेभ्यो ज्ञानविमुक्तभक्तिपरमाः प्रेमैकनिष्ठास्ततः ।
तेभ्यस्ताः पशुपालपङ्कजदृशस्ताभ्योऽपि सा राधिका
प्रेष्ठा तद्वदियं तदीयसरसी तां नाश्रयेत्कः कृती ॥१०॥

karmibhyaḥ parito hareḥ priyatayā vyaktiṁ yayur jñāninas
tebhyo jñāna-vimukta-bhakti-paramāḥ premaika-niṣṭhās tataḥ
tebhyas tāḥ paśu-pāla-paṅkaja-dṛśas tābhyo 'pi sā rādhikā
preṣṭhā tadvad iyaṁ tadīya-sarasī tāṁ nāśrayet kaḥ kṛtī

karmibhyaḥ—than all fruitive workers; *paritaḥ*—in all respects; *hareḥ*—by the Supreme Personality of Godhead; *priyatayā*—because of being favored; *vyaktim yayuḥ*—it is said in the *śāstra; jñāninaḥ*—those advanced in knowledge; *tebhyaḥ*—superior to them; *jñāna-vimukta*—liberated by knowledge; *bhakti-paramāḥ*—those engaged in devotional service; *prema-eka-niṣṭhāḥ*—those who have attained pure love of God; *tataḥ*—superior to them; *tebhyaḥ*—better than them; *tāḥ*—they; *paśu-pāla-paṅkaja-dṛśaḥ*—the *gopīs,* who are always dependent on Kṛṣṇa, the cowherd boy; *tābhyaḥ*—above all of them; *api*—certainly; *sā*—She; *rādhikā*—Śrīmatī Rādhikā; *preṣṭhā*—very dear; *tadvat*—similarly; *iyam*—this; *tadīya-sarasī*—Her lake, Śrī Rādhā-kuṇḍa; *tām*—Rādhā-kuṇḍa; *na*—not; *āśrayet*—would take shelter of; *kaḥ*—who; *kṛtī*—most fortunate.

TRANSLATION

In the śāstra it is said that of all types of fruitive workers, he who is advanced in knowledge of the higher values of life is favored by the Supreme Lord Hari. Out of many such people who are advanced in knowledge [jñānīs], one who is practically liberated by virtue of his knowledge may take to devotional service. He is superior to the others. However, one who has actually attained prema, pure love of Kṛṣṇa, is superior to him. The gopīs are exalted above all the advanced devotees because they are always totally dependent upon Śrī Kṛṣṇa, the transcendental cowherd boy. Among the gopīs, Śrīmatī Rādhārāṇī is the most dear to Kṛṣṇa. Her kuṇḍa [lake] is as profoundly dear to Lord Kṛṣṇa as this most beloved of the gopīs. Who, then, will not reside at Rādhā-kuṇḍa and, in a spiritual body surcharged with ecstatic devotional feelings [aprākṛta-bhāva], render loving service to the divine couple Śrī Śrī Rādhā-Govinda, who perform Their aṣṭakālīya-līlā, Their eternal eightfold daily pastimes? Indeed, those who execute devotional service on the banks of Rādhā-kuṇḍa are the most fortunate people in the universe.

PURPORT

At the present moment almost everyone is engaged in some kind of fruitive activity. Those who are desirous of gaining material profits by working are called *karmīs,* or fruitive workers. All living entities within this material world have come under the spell of *māyā*. This is described in the *Viṣṇu Purāṇa* (6.7.61):

viṣṇu-śaktiḥ parā proktā
kṣetrajñākhyā tathā parā
avidyā-karma-saṁjñānyā
tṛtīyā śaktir iṣyate

Sages have divided the energies of the Supreme Personality of Godhead into three categories—namely, the spiritual energy, marginal energy and material energy. The material energy is considered to be the third-class energy (*tṛtīyā śaktiḥ*). Those living beings within the jurisdiction of the material energy sometimes engage themselves like dogs and hogs in working very hard simply for sense gratification. However, in this life, or, after executing pious activities, in the next life, some *karmīs* become strongly attracted to performing various kinds of sacrifices mentioned in the *Vedas*. Thus on the strength of their pious merit, they are elevated to heavenly planets. Actually those who perform sacrifices strictly according to Vedic injunctions are elevated to the moon and planets above the moon. As mentioned in the *Bhagavad-gītā* (9.21), *kṣīṇe puṇye martya-lokaṁ viśanti:* after exhausting the results of their so-called pious activities, they return to the earth, which is called *martya-loka,* the place of death. Although such persons may be elevated to the heavenly planets by their pious activities and although they may enjoy life there for many thousands of years, they nonetheless must return to this planet when the results of their pious activities are exhausted.

This is the position of all *karmīs,* including those who act piously and those who act impiously. On this planet we find many businessmen, politicians and others who are simply interested in material happiness. They attempt to earn money by all means, not considering whether such means are pious or impious. Such people are called *karmīs,* or gross materialists. Among the *karmīs* are some *vikarmīs,* people who act without the guidance of Vedic knowledge. Those who act on the basis of Vedic knowledge perform sacrifices for the satisfaction of Lord Viṣṇu and to receive benedictions from Him. In this way they are elevated to higher planetary systems. Such *karmīs* are superior to the *vikarmīs,* for they are faithful to the directions of the *Vedas* and are certainly dear to Kṛṣṇa. In the *Bhagavad-gītā* (4.11), Kṛṣṇa says: *ye yathā māṁ prapadyante tāṁs tathaiva bhajāmy aham.* "In whatever way one surrenders unto Me, I reward him accordingly." Kṛṣṇa is so kind that He fulfilled the desires of the *karmīs* and *jñānīs,* what to speak of the *bhaktas.* Although the *karmīs* are sometimes elevated to higher planetary systems, as long as they remain attached to fruitive activities they must accept new material bodies after death. If one acts piously, he can attain a new body among the demigods in the higher planetary systems, or he may attain some other position in which he can enjoy a higher standard of material happiness. On the other hand, those who are engaged in impious activities are degraded and take birth as animals, trees and plants. Thus those fruitive actors who do not care for the Vedic directions (*vikarmīs*) are not appreciated by learned saintly persons. As stated in *Śrīmad-Bhāgavatam* (5.5.4):

nūnaṁ pramattaḥ kurute vikarma
yad indriya-prītaya āpṛṇoti
na sādhu manye yata ātmano 'yam
asann api kleśada āsa dehaḥ

"Materialists who work hard like dogs and hogs simply for sense gratification are actually mad. They simply perform all kinds of abominable activities simply for sense gratification. Materialistic activities are not at all worthy of an intelligent man, for as a result of such activities one gets a material body, which is full of misery." The purpose of human life is to get out of the threefold miserable conditions, which are concomitant with material existence. Unfortunately, fruitive workers are mad to earn money and acquire temporary material comforts by all means; therefore they risk being degraded to lower species of life. Materialists foolishly make many plans to become happy in this material world. They do not stop to consider that they will live only for a certain number of years, out of which they must spend the major portion acquiring money for sense gratification. Ultimately such activities end in death. Materialists do not consider that after giving up the body they may become embodied as lower animals, plants or trees. Thus all their activities simply defeat the purpose of life. Not only are they born ignorant, but they act on the platform of ignorance, thinking that they are getting material benefits in the shape of skyscraper buildings, big cars, honorable positions and so on. The materialists do not know that in the next life they will be degraded and that all their activities simply serve as *parābhava,* their defeat. This is the verdict of *Śrīmad-Bhāgavatam* (5.5.5): *parābhavas tāvad abodha-jātaḥ.*

One should therefore be eager to understand the science of the soul (*ātma-tattva*). Unless one comes to the platform of *ātma-tattva,* by which one understands that the soul and not the body is oneself, one remains on the platform of ignorance. Out of thousands and even millions of ignorant people who are wasting their time simply gratifying their senses, one may come to the platform of knowledge and understand higher values of life. Such a person is called a *jñānī*. The *jñānī* knows that fruitive activities will bind him to material existence and cause him to transmigrate from one kind of body to another. As indicated in *Śrīmad-Bhāgavatam* by the term *śarīra-bandha* (bound to bodily existence), as long as one maintains any conception of sense enjoyment, his mind will be absorbed in *karma*, fruitive activity, and this will oblige him to transmigrate from one body to another.

Thus a *jñānī* is considered superior to a *karmī* because he at least refrains from the blind activities of sense enjoyment. This is the verdict of the Supreme Personality of Godhead. However, although a *jñānī* may be liberated from the ignorance of the *karmīs*, if he does not come to the platform of devotional service he is still considered to be in ignorance (*avidyā*). Although such a person may be accepted as a *jñānī*, or one advanced in knowledge, his knowledge is considered impure because he has no information of devotional service and thus neglects the direct worship of the lotus feet of the Lord.

When a *jñānī* takes to devotional service, he rapidly becomes superior to an ordinary *jñānī*. Such an advanced person is described in the present verse of *Śrī Upadeśāmṛta* as *jñāna-vimukta-bhakti-parama*. How a *jñānī* takes to devotional service is mentioned in the *Bhagavad-gītā* (7.19), wherein Kṛṣṇa says:

bahūnāṁ janmanām ante
jñānavān māṁ prapadyate

vāsudevaḥ sarvam iti
sa mahātmā sudurlabhaḥ

"After many births and deaths, he who is actually in knowledge surrenders unto Me, knowing Me to be the cause of all causes and all that is. Such a great soul is very rare."

After taking to devotional service under the regulative principles, a person may come to the platform of spontaneous love of Godhead, following in the footsteps of great devotees like Nārada and Sanaka and Sanātana. The Supreme Personality of Godhead then recognizes him to be superior. The devotees who have developed love of Godhead are certainly in an exalted position.

Of all these devotees, the *gopīs* are recognized as superior because they do not know anything other than satisfying Kṛṣṇa. Nor do the *gopīs* expect any return from Kṛṣṇa. Indeed, sometimes Kṛṣṇa puts them into extreme suffering by separating Himself from them. Nonetheless, they cannot forget Kṛṣṇa. When Kṛṣṇa left Vṛndāvana for Mathurā, the *gopīs* became most dejected and spent the rest of their lives simply crying in separation from Kṛṣṇa. This means that in one sense they were never actually separated from Kṛṣṇa. There is no difference between thinking of Kṛṣṇa and associating with Him. Rather, *vipralambha-sevā,* thinking of Kṛṣṇa in separation, as Śrī Caitanya Mahāprabhu did, is far better than serving Kṛṣṇa directly. Thus of all the devotees who have developed unalloyed devotional love for Kṛṣṇa, the *gopīs* are most exalted, and out of all these exalted *gopīs,* Śrīmatī Rādhārāṇī is the highest. No one can excel the devotional service of Śrīmatī

Rādhārāṇī. Indeed, even Kṛṣṇa cannot understand the attitude of Śrīmatī Rādhārāṇī; therefore He took Her position and appeared as Śrī Caitanya Mahāprabhu, just to understand Her transcendental feelings.

In this way Śrīla Rūpa Gosvāmī gradually concludes that Śrīmatī Rādhārāṇī is the most exalted devotee of Kṛṣṇa and that Her *kuṇḍa* (lake), Śrī Rādhā-kuṇḍa, is the most exalted place. This is verified in a quotation from the *Laghu-bhāgavatāmṛta* (*Uttara-khaṇḍa* 45), as quoted in the *Caitanya-caritāmṛta:*

yathā rādhā priyā viṣṇos
tasyāḥ kuṇḍaṁ priyaṁ tathā
sarva-gopīṣu saivaikā
viṣṇor atyanta-vallabhā

"Just as Śrīmatī Rādhārāṇī is dear to the Supreme Lord Kṛṣṇa [Viṣṇu], so Her bathing place [Rādhā-kuṇḍa] is equally dear to Kṛṣṇa. Among all the *gopīs,* She alone stands supreme as the Lord's most beloved."

Therefore everyone interested in Kṛṣṇa consciousness should ultimately take shelter of Rādhā-kuṇḍa and execute devotional service there throughout one's life. This is the conclusion of Rūpa Gosvāmī in the tenth verse of the *Upadeśāmṛta*.

TEXT ELEVEN

कृष्णस्योच्चैः प्रणयवसतिः प्रेयसीभ्योऽपि राधा
कुण्डं चास्या मुनिभिरभितस्तादृगेव व्यधायि ।

यत्प्रेष्ठैरप्यलमसुलभं किं पुनर्भक्तिभाजां
तत्प्रेमेदं सकृदपि सरः स्नातुराविष्करोति ॥११॥

kṛṣṇasyoccaiḥ praṇaya-vasatiḥ preyasībhyo 'pi rādhā
kuṇḍaṁ cāsyā munibhir abhitas tādṛg eva vyadhāyi
yat preṣṭhair apy alam asulabhaṁ kiṁ punar bhakti-bhājāṁ
tat premedaṁ sakṛd api saraḥ snātur āviṣkaroti

kṛṣṇasya—of Lord Śrī Kṛṣṇa; *uccaiḥ*—very highly; *praṇaya-vasatiḥ*—object of love; *preyasībhyaḥ*—out of the many lovable *gopīs; api*—certainly; *rādhā*—Śrīmatī Rādhārāṇī; *kuṇḍam*—lake; *ca*—also; *asyāḥ*—of Her; *munibhiḥ*—by great sages; *abhitaḥ*—in all respects; *tādṛk eva*—similarly; *vyadhāyi*—is described; *yat*—which; *preṣṭhaiḥ*—by the most advanced devotees; *api*—even; *alam*—enough; *asulabham*—difficult to obtain; *kim*—what; *punaḥ*—again; *bhakti-bhājām*—for persons engaged in devotional service; *tat*—that; *prema*—love of Godhead; *idam*—this; *sakṛt*—once; *api*—even; *saraḥ*—lake; *snātuḥ*—of one who has bathed; *āviṣkaroti*—arouses.

TRANSLATION

Of the many objects of favored delight and of all the lovable damsels of Vrajabhūmi, Śrīmatī Rādhārāṇī is certainly the most treasured object of Kṛṣṇa's love. And, in every respect, Her divine kuṇḍa is described by great sages as similarly dear to Him. Undoubtedly Rādhā-kuṇḍa is very rarely attained even by the

great devotees; therefore it is even more difficult for ordinary devotees to attain. If one simply bathes once within those holy waters, one's pure love of Kṛṣṇa is fully aroused.

PURPORT

Why is Rādhā-kuṇḍa so exalted? The lake is so exalted because it belongs to Śrīmatī Rādhārāṇī, who is the most beloved object of Śrī Kṛṣṇa. Among all the *gopīs,* She is the most beloved. Similarly, Her lake, Śrī Rādhā-kuṇḍa, is also described by great sages as the lake that is as dear to Kṛṣṇa as Rādhā Herself. Indeed, Kṛṣṇa's love for Rādhā-kuṇḍa and for Śrīmatī Rādhārāṇī is the same in all respects. Rādhā-kuṇḍa is very rarely attained, even by great personalities fully engaged in devotional service, what to speak of ordinary devotees who are engaged only in the practice of *vaidhī-bhakti.*

It is stated that a devotee will at once develop pure love of Kṛṣṇa in the wake of the *gopīs* if he once takes a bath in Rādhā-kuṇḍa. Śrīla Rūpa Gosvāmī recommends that even if one cannot live permanently on the banks of Rādhā-kuṇḍa, he should at least take a bath in the lake as many times as possible. This is a most important item in the execution of devotional service. Śrīla Bhaktivinoda Ṭhākura writes in this connection that Śrī Rādhā-kuṇḍa is the most select place for those interested in advancing their devotional service in the wake of the lady friends (*sakhīs*) and confidential serving maids (*mañjarīs*) of Śrīmatī Rādhārāṇī. Living entities who are eager to return home to the transcendental kingdom of God, Goloka Vṛndāvana, by means of attaining their spiritual bodies (*siddha-deha*) should live at Rādhā-kuṇḍa, take shelter of the confidential serving maids of Śrī Rādhā and under their direction engage constantly in Her service. This is the most exalted method for those engaged in devotional service under the protection of Śrī Caitanya Mahāprabhu. In this connection Śrīla Bhaktisiddhānta Sarasvatī Ṭhākura writes that even great sages and great devotees like Nārada and Sanaka do not get an opportunity to come to Rādhā-kuṇḍa to take their baths. What, then, to speak of ordinary devotees? If, by great fortune, one gets an opportunity to come to Rādhā-kuṇḍa and bathe even once, he can develop his transcendental love for Kṛṣṇa, exactly as the *gopīs* did. It is also recommended that one should live on the banks of Rādhā-kuṇḍa and should be absorbed in the loving service of the Lord. One should bathe there regularly and give up all material conceptions, taking shelter of Śrī Rādhā and Her assistant *gopīs*. If one is thus constantly engaged during his lifetime, after giving up the body he will return back to Godhead to serve Śrī Rādhā in the same way as he contemplated during his life on the banks of Rādhā-kuṇḍa. The conclusion is that to live on the banks of Rādhā-kuṇḍa and to bathe there daily constitute the highest perfection of devotional service. It is a difficult position to attain, even for great sages and devotees like Nārada. Thus there is no limit to the glory of Śrī Rādhā-kuṇḍa. By serving Rādhā-kuṇḍa, one can get an opportunity to become an assistant of Śrīmatī Rādhārāṇī under the eternal guidance of the *gopīs*.

APPENDIXES

THE AUTHOR

His Divine Grace A. C. Bhaktivedanta Swami Prabhupāda appeared in this world in 1896 in Calcutta, India. He first met his spiritual master, Śrīla Bhaktisiddhānta Sarasvatī Gosvāmī, in Calcutta in 1922. Bhaktisiddhānta Sarasvatī, a prominent religious scholar and the founder of sixty-four Gauḍīya Maṭhas (Vedic institutes), liked this educated young man and convinced him to dedicate his life to teaching Vedic knowledge. Śrīla Prabhupāda became his student and, in 1933, his formally initiated disciple.

At their first meeting, in 1922, Śrīla Bhaktisiddhānta Sarasvatī requested Śrīla Prabhupāda to broadcast Vedic knowledge in English. In the years that followed, Śrīla Prabhupāda wrote a commentary on the *Bhagavad-gītā*, assisted the Gauḍīya Maṭha in its work, and, in 1944, started *Back to Godhead*, an English fortnightly magazine. Single-handedly, Śrīla Prabhupāda edited it, typed the manuscripts, checked the galley proofs, and even distributed the individual copies. The magazine is now being continued by his followers.

In 1950 Śrīla Prabhupāda retired from married life, adopting the *vānaprastha* (retired) order to devote more time to his studies and writing. He traveled to the holy city of Vṛndāvana, where he lived in humble circumstances in the historic temple of Rādhā-Dāmodara. There he engaged for several years in deep study and writing. He accepted the renounced order of life (*sannyāsa*) in 1959. At Rādhā-Dāmodara, Śrīla Prabhupāda began work on his life's masterpiece: a multivolume commentated translation of the eighteen-thousand-verse *Śrīmad-Bhāgavatam* (*Bhāgavata Purāṇa*). He also wrote *Easy Journey to Other Planets.*

After publishing three volumes of *Śrīmad-Bhāgavatam,* Śrīla Prabhupāda came to the United States, in September 1965, to fulfill the mission of his spiritual master. Subsequently, His Divine Grace wrote more than fifty volumes of authoritative commentated translations and summary studies of the philosophical and religious classics of India.

When he first arrived by freighter in New York City, Śrīla Prabhupāda was practically penniless. Only after almost a year of great difficulty did he establish the International Society for Krishna Consciousness, in July of 1966. Before he passed away on November 14, 1977, he had guided the Society and seen it grow to a worldwide confederation of more than one hundred *āśramas,* schools, temples, institutes and farm communities.

In 1972 His Divine Grace introduced the Vedic system of primary and secondary education in the West by founding the *gurukula* school in Dallas, Texas. Since then his disciples have established similar schools throughout the United States and the rest of the world.

Śrīla Prabhupāda also inspired the construction of several large international cultural centers in India. At Śrīdhāma Māyāpur, in West Bengal, devotees are building a spiritual city centered on a magnificent temple—an ambitious project for which construction will extend over many years to come. In Vṛndāvana are the Kṛṣṇa-Balarāma Temple and International Guesthouse, *gurukula* school, and Śrīla Prabhupāda Memorial and Museum. There are also major temples and cultural centers in Mumbai, New Delhi, Ahmedabad, Siliguri, and Ujjain. Other centers are planned in many important locations on the Indian subcontinent.

Śrīla Prabhupāda's most significant contribution, however, is his books. Highly respected by scholars for their authority, depth, and clarity, they are used as textbooks in numerous college courses. His writings have been translated into over fifty languages. The Bhaktivedanta Book Trust, established in 1972 to publish the works of His Divine Grace, has thus become the world's largest publisher of books in the field of Indian religion and philosophy.

In just twelve years, despite his advanced age, Śrīla Prabhupāda circled the globe fourteen times on lecture tours that took him to six continents. In spite of such a vigorous schedule, Śrīla Prabhupāda continued to write prolifically. His writings constitute a veritable library of Vedic philosophy, religion, literature, and culture.

REFERENCES

Bhagavad-gītā, 16, 29, 31, 35, 36, 37–38, 41, 60, 61–62, 73–74, 83, 84, 86–87

Bhakti-rasāmṛta-sindhu (Rūpa Gosvāmī), 27–28, 30, 57, 74, 75

Caitanya-caritāmṛta (Kṛṣṇadāsa Kavirāja), 5, 11, 29–30, 41, 51, 53, 55, 56, 71–72, 76, 80, 88

Īśopaniṣad, 25

Laghu-bhāgavatāmṛta (Rūpa Gosvāmī), 88

Muṇḍaka Upaniṣad, 29

Prema-vivarta (Jagadānanda Paṇḍita), 12–13

Śikṣāṣṭaka (Caitanya Mahāprabhu), 6, 42

Śrīmad-Bhāgavatam, 2, 3, 8, 13–14, 19, 22, 35, 37, 44, 49, 52, 84–85

Viṣṇu Purāṇa, 82–83

GLOSSARY

A

Ācārya—a spiritual master; one who teaches by example.
Ādhibhautika-kleśa—sufferings caused by other living entities.
Ādhidaivika-kleśa—sufferings caused by supernatural occurrences.
Ādhyātmika-kleśa—sufferings caused by one's own body and mind.
Ahaṅkāra—false ego, where spirit meets matter.
Antaraṅga-śakti—the internal, spiritual potency of the Supreme Lord.
Āśrama—a spiritual order of life.
Aṣṭakālīya-līlā—the eternal eightfold daily pastimes of Rādhā-Govinda.
Ātma-tattva—the science of the soul.
Atyāhāra—collecting or eating more than necessary.
Avidyā—ignorance.

B

Bahiraṅga-śakti—the external, material potency of the Supreme Lord.

Bhajana-kriyā—the practice of devotional service.
Bhaktas—devotees.
Bhakti—devotional service to the Supreme Lord.
Bhāva—the preliminary stage of love of God.
Bhukti-kāmīs—persons interested in material happiness.
Brahmā—the first created living being. He creates the planets and the bodies for all species of life.
Brahmacārī—a celibate student under the care of a spiritual master.
Brahmacarya—the vow of strict abstinence from sex indulgence.
Brāhmaṇa—a person wise in Vedic knowledge, fixed in goodness, and knowledgeable of Brahman, the Absolute Truth; a member of the first Vedic social order.

D

Dāsya-rasa—the attitude of servitorship toward the Supreme Lord.
Dīkṣā—spiritual initiation.
Durātmā—a cripple-minded person under the control of the external potency of the Supreme Lord.

E

Ekādaśī—a special day for increased remembrance of Kṛṣṇa that comes on the eleventh day after both the full and new moon. Abstinence from grains and beans is prescribed.

G

Go-dāsa—a servant of the senses.
Gopīs—Kṛṣṇa's cowherd girlfriends.
Gosvāmīs of Vṛndāvana—*See:* Six Gosvāmīs of Vṛndāvana.

H

Hari-nāma initiation—initiation into the chanting of the Hare Kṛṣṇa *mahā-mantra.*
Hātī-mātā—the "mad elephant" offense, one committed against a Vaiṣṇava, which destroys one's devotional creeper.

I

Indra—the king of the demigods.

J

Jana-saṅga—association with persons not interested in Kṛṣṇa consciousness.
Janmāṣṭamī—Kṛṣṇa's appearance day.
Japa-mālā—string of 108 prayer beads for chanting the Hare Kṛṣṇa *mahā-mantra.*
Jīvātmās—the minute living entities, who are eternal individual souls, part and parcel of the Supreme Lord.
Jñānī—one engaged in the cultivation of knowledge.

K

Kaniṣṭha-adhikārī—a neophyte devotee, whose faith is not firm.

Karmīs—fruitive workers.

Kīrtana—glorification of the Supreme Lord.

Krodha—anger.

Kṛṣṇa-kathā—topics spoken by or about Kṛṣṇa.

L

Lakṣmī—the goddess of fortune.

M

Mādhurya-rasa—the mellow of conjugal love with the Supreme Lord, as best exhibited by the *gopīs*.

Madhyama-adhikārī—a second-class devotee, who has received spiritual initiation and is fully engaged in devotional service.

Mahā-bhāgavata—a greatly advanced devotee.

Mahā-mantra—the great chanting for deliverance: Hare Kṛṣṇa, Hare Kṛṣṇa, Kṛṣṇa Kṛṣṇa, Hare Hare/ Hare Rāma, Hare Rāma, Rāma Rāma, Hare Hare.

Mahātmā—a great soul, or devotee.

Maṅgala-ārati—the early-morning ceremony to greet the Lord.

Mañjarīs—maidservants of the *gopīs*.

Mano-vega—the urges of the restless mind.

Mantra—a pure sound vibration that, when chanted, delivers the mind from material contamination.

Martya-loka—the place of repeated death, i.e., the earth planet.

Māyā—(*mā*—not; *yā*—this) illusion; forgetfulness of one's relationship with Kṛṣṇa.

Mukti-kāmīs—persons desiring liberation by merging into the impersonal existence of Brahman.

P

Paramahaṁsas—the topmost swanlike devotees.

Patita-pāvana—deliverer of the fallen souls.

Prajalpa—unnecessary talking.

Prākṛta-sahajiyās—materialistic pseudodevotees.

Prasādam—the remnants of food offered to Kṛṣṇa.

Prayāsa—unnecessary endeavor.

Prāyaścitta—atonement.

Prema—matured pure love of Kṛṣṇa.

R

Rāga-bhakti—devotional service in spontaneous love.

Rāgānuga-bhakti—spontaneous devotional service in which the devotee follows in the footsteps of one of the eternal associates of Kṛṣṇa in Vṛndāvana.

Rasa—the particular loving mood or attitude relished in the exchange of love with the Supreme Lord.

S

Sādhu—a saintly person, or devotee.

Sādhya—the stage of having achieved God realization.

Sakhya-rasa—the relationship with the Supreme Lord in friendship.

Samādhi—the state of trance when the consciousness is absorbed in the Supreme.

Saṅkīrtana—congregational chanting of the holy names.

Sannyāsa—the renounced order of life.

Śānta-rasa—the passive or neutral relationship with the Supreme Lord.

Śāstras—the revealed scriptures.

Siddhi-kāmīs—persons desiring the perfection of mystic *yoga*.

Six Gosvāmīs of Vṛndāvana—Śrī Sanātana Gosvāmī, Śrī Rūpa Gosvāmī, Śrī Raghunātha Bhaṭṭa Gosvāmī, Śrī Raghunātha Dāsa Gosvāmī, Śrī Jīva Gosvāmī and Śrī Gopāla Bhaṭṭa Gosvāmī. They are the principal followers of Śrī Caitanya Mahāprabhu.

Smaraṇa—the devotional process of remembering Kṛṣṇa's name, form, qualities, and pastimes.

Śraddhāvān—a faithful person.

Śravaṇa—the devotional process of hearing Kṛṣṇa's name and descriptions of His form, qualities and pastimes.

Svāmī—one who controls his mind and the senses; a person in the renounced order of life.

T

Tapasya—voluntarily accepting some material inconvenience to progress in spiritual life.

Taṭasthā-śakti—the marginal potency of the Supreme Lord, comprising the minute living entities.

Tyāgīs—those in the renounced order of life.

U

Utsāha—enthusiasm.
Uttama-adhikārī—a first-class devotee, who is very advanced in devotional service and has attained pure Kṛṣṇa consciousness.
Uttamā-bhakti—unalloyed devotion unto the Supreme Personality of Godhead.

V

Vaidhī-bhakti—following the principles of regulated devotional service by the order of the spiritual master or according to the injunctions of the revealed scriptures.
Vaiṣṇava-aparādha—an offense against a devotee of the Lord.
Vātsalya-rasa—the parental relationship with the Supreme Lord.
Vikarmīs—fruitive actors who don't follow the Vedic directions.
Vipralambha-sevā—thinking of Kṛṣṇa in separation.
Viśuddha-sattva—the platform of pure goodness.

Y

Yoga-siddhi—mystic perfection.

SANSKRIT PRONUNCIATION GUIDE

Throughout the centuries, the Sanskrit language has been written in a variety of alphabets. The mode of writing most widely used throughout India, however, is called *devanāgarī*, which means, literally, the writing used in "the cities of the demigods." The *devanāgarī* alphabet consists of forty-eight characters: thirteen vowels and thirty-five consonants. Ancient Sanskrit grammarians arranged this alphabet according to practical linguistic principles, and this order has been accepted by all Western scholars. The system of transliteration used in this book conforms to a system that scholars have accepted to indicate the pronunciation of each Sanskrit sound.

Vowels

अ a आ ā इ i ई ī उ u ऊ ū ऋ ṛ
ॠ ṝ ऌ ḷ ए e ऐ ai ओ o औ au

Consonants

Gutturals:	क ka	ख kha	ग ga	घ gha	ङ ṅa
Palatals:	च ca	छ cha	ज ja	झ jha	ञ ña
Cerebrals:	ट ṭa	ठ ṭha	ड ḍa	ढ ḍha	ण ṇa
Dentals:	त ta	थ tha	द da	ध dha	न na
Labials:	प pa	फ pha	ब ba	भ bha	म ma
Semivowels:	य ya	र ra	ल la	व va	
Sibilants:	श śa	ष ṣa	स sa		
Aspirate:	ह ha	Anusvāra: ं ṁ		Visarga: ः ḥ	

Numerals

० – 0 १ – 1 २ – 2 ३ – 3 ४ – 4 ५ – 5 ६ – 6 ७ – 7 ८ – 8 ९ – 9

The vowels appear as follows in conjunction with a consonant:

ा ā ि i ी ī ु u ू ū ृ ṛ ॄ ṝ े e ै ai ो o ौ au

For example: क ka का kā कि ki की kī कु ku कू kū कृ kṛ कॄ kṝ कॢ kḷ के ke कै kai को ko कौ kau

Generally two or more consonants in conjunction are written together in a special form, as for example: क्ष kṣa त्र tra
The vowel "a" is implied after a consonant with no vowel symbol. The symbol *virāma* (्) indicates that there is no final vowel: क्

The vowels are pronounced as follows:

a — as in but
ā — as in far but held twice as long as **a**
i — as in pin
ī — as in pique but held twice as long is **i**
u — as in push
ū — as in rule but held twice as long as **u**

ṛ — as in **ri**m
ṝ — as in **ree**d but held twice as long as **ṛ**
ḷ — as in happily
e — as in they
ai — as in aisle
o — as in go
au — as in how

The consonants are pronounced as follows:

Gutturals
(pronounced from the throat)

k — as in kite
kh — as in Eckhart
g — as in give
gh — as in dig-hard
ṅ — as in sing

Palatals
(pronounced with the middle of the tongue against the palate)

c — as in **ch**air
ch — as in staun**ch-h**eart
j — as in joy
jh — as in hedgehog
ñ — as in canyon

Cerebrals
(pronounced with the tip of the tongue against the roof of the mouth)
ṭ — as in **t**ub
ṭh — as in ligh**t-h**eart
ḍ — as in **d**ove
ḍh — as in re**d-h**ot
ṅ — as in si**ng**

Dentals
(pronounced like the cerebrals but with the tongue against the teeth)
t — as in **t**ub
th — as in ligh**t-h**eart
d — as in **d**ove
dh — as in re**d-h**ot
n — as in **n**ut

Labials
(pronounced with the lips)
p — as in **p**ine
ph — as in u**p-h**ill (not f)
b — as in **b**ird
bh — as in ru**b-h**ard
m — as in **m**other

Semivowels
y — as in **y**es
r — as in **r**un
l — as in **l**ight
v — as in **v**ine, except when preceded in the same syllable by a consonant; then as in s**w**an

Sibilants
ś — as in the German word spre**ch**en
ṣ — as in **sh**ine
s — as in **s**un

Aspirate
h — as in **h**ome

Visarga
ḥ — a final h-sound: **aḥ** is pronounced like **aha**; **iḥ** like **ihi**.

Anusvara
ṁ — a resonant nasal sound as in the French word *bo*n

There is no strong accentuation of syllables in Sanskrit, or pausing between words in a line. There is only a flowing of short and long syllables (the long twice as long as the short). A long syllable is one whose vowel is long (**ā, ī, ū, ṝ, e, ai, o, au**) or whose short vowel is followed by more than one consonant. The letters **ḥ** and **ṁ** count as consonants. Aspirated consonants (consonants followed by an **h**) count as single consonants.

INDEX OF SANSKRIT VERSES

This index constitutes a complete alphabetical listing of each line of the verses in *Śrī Upadeśāmṛta*. In the first column the transliteration is given, and in the second and third columns, respectively, the verse reference and page number for each verse are to be found.

GENERAL INDEX

Numerals in bold type indicate references to *Śrī Upadeśāmṛta's* verses. Numerals in regular type are references to its purports.

A

Absolute Truth
  inquiry into, as purpose of life, 20
  learning science of, 52
  See also: Kṛṣṇa; Supreme Lord
Ācāryas
  executing principles given by, 33, 34
  following in footsteps of, 27, 46
  See also: Pure devotees; Spiritual master
Activity (Activities)
  based on sense gratification, 16
  devotional, performance of, 31, 32, 39
  frivolous, examples of, 20–21
  of *karmīs* and *jñānīs,* 22
  of Kṛṣṇa, 66
  material, devotee has no interest in, 37
  materialistic, result of, 85
  nonpermanent, becoming callous to, 35
  pious, executed by *karmīs,* 83
  regulative, performance of, 33
  sinful, can't be counteracted by pious activities, 3
  which spoil devotional service, 15
Activity (*continued*)
  subsidiary, performed via devotional service, 56
  as substance of devotional service, 27, 28
  transcendental, devotional service as, 34
  of Vaiṣṇava, can't be viewed materially, 64
  Vaiṣṇavas distinguished on basis of, 65
  See also: Fruitive activities
Advaita Prabhu, descendants of, as *gosvāmīs,* 62, 63
Ānandāmbudhi-vardhanam
  verse quoted, 42
Anger
  as agitation of mind, 9
  controlled by *svāmī,* 13
  tolerating urge of, 1, 5–6
Animals
  distinction between humans &, 20
  have no economic problems, 18
  have no religion, 44
  purification of, 42–43
  taking birth as, 84
Anuvṛtti
  cited on over-endeavoring for knowledge, 21
  cited on three kinds of urges, 8

M

The International Society for Krishna Consciousness

Founder-*Ācārya:* His Divine Grace A.C. Bhaktivedanta Swami Prabhupāda

CENTERS AROUND THE WORLD

NORTH AMERICA

CANADA

Brampton-Mississauga, Ontario – Unit 20, 1030 Kamato Dr., L4W 4B6/ Tel. (416) 840-6587 or (905) 826-1290/ iskconbrampton@gmail.com

Calgary, Alberta – 313 Fourth St. N.E., T2E 3S3/ Tel. (403) 265-3302/ Fax: (403) 547-0795/ vamanstones@shaw.ca

Edmonton, Alberta – 9353 35th Ave. NW, T6E 5R5/ Tel. (780) 439-9999/ harekrishna.edmonton@gmail.com

Montreal, Quebec – 1626 Pie IX Blvd., H1V 2C5/ Tel. & fax: (514) 521-1301/ iskconmontreal@gmail.com

◆ **Ottawa, Ontario** – 212 Somerset St. E., K1N 6V4/ Tel. (613) 565-6544/ Fax: (613) 565-2575/ iskconottawa@sympatico.ca

Regina, Saskatchewan – 1279 Retallack St., S4T 2H8/ Tel. (306) 525-0002 or -6461/ jagadishadas@yahoo.com

Scarborough, Ontario – 3500 McNicoll Avenue, Unit #3, M1V4C7/ Tel. (647) 955-0415/ iskconscarborough@hotmail.com

Toronto, Ontario – 243 Avenue Rd., M5R 2J6/ Tel. (416) 922-5415/ Fax: (416) 922-1021/ toronto@iskcon.net

Vancouver, B.C. – 5462 S.E. Marine Dr., Burnaby V5J 3G8/ Tel. (604) 433-9728/ Fax: (604) 648-8715/ akrura@krishna.com

RURAL COMMUNITY

Ashcroft, B.C. – Saranagati Dhama, Venables Valley (mail: P.O. Box 99, VOK 1A0)/ Tel. (250) 457-7438/ Fax: (250) 453-9306/ iskconsaranagati@hotmail.com

U.S.A.

◆ **Atlanta, Georgia** – 1287 South Ponce de Leon Ave. N.E., 30306/ Tel. & fax: (404) 377-8680/ admin@atlantaharekrishnas.com

Austin, Texas – 10700 Jonwood Way, 78753/ Tel. (512) 835-2121/ Fax: (512) 835-8479/ sda@backtohome.com

Baltimore, Maryland –200 Bloomsbury Ave., Catonsville, 21228/ Tel. (410) 719-1776/ Fax: (410) 799-0642/ info@baltimorekrishna.com

Berkeley, California – 2334 Stuart St., 94705/ Tel. (510) 649-8619/ rajan416@yahoo.com

Boise, Idaho – 1615 Martha St., 83706/ Tel. (208) 344-4274/ boise_temple@yahoo.com

Boston, Massachusetts – 72 Commonwealth Ave., 02116/ Tel. (617) 247-8611/ Fax: (617) 909-5181/ darukrishna@iskconboston.org

Chicago, Illinois – 1716 W. Lunt Ave., 60626/ Tel. (773) 973-0900/ Fax: (773) 973-0526/ chicagoiskcon@yahoo.com

Columbus, Ohio – 379 W. Eighth Ave., 43201/ Tel. (614) 421-1661/ Fax: (614) 294-0545/ rmanjari@sbcglobal.net

◆ **Dallas, Texas** – 5430 Gurley Ave., 75223/ Tel. (214) 827-6330/ Fax: (214) 823-7264/ txkrishnas@aol.com; restaurant: vegetariantaste@aol.com

◆ **Denver, Colorado** – 1400 Cherry St., 80220/ Tel. (303) 333-5461/ Fax: (303) 321-9052/ info@krishnadenver.com

Detroit, Michigan – 383 Lenox Ave., 48215/ Tel. (313) 824-6000/ gaurangi108@hotmail.com

Gainesville, Florida – 214 N.W. 14th St., 32603/ Tel. (352) 336-4183/ Fax: (352) 379-2927/ kalakantha.acbsp@pamho.net

Hartford, Connecticut – 1683 Main St., E. Hartford 06108/ Tel. & fax: (860) 289-7252/ pyari@sbcglobal.net

◆ **Honolulu, Hawaii** – 51 Coelho Way, 96817/ Tel. (808) 595-4913/ rama108@bigfoot.com

Houston, Texas – 1320 W. 34th St., 77018/ Tel. (713) 686-4482/ Fax: (713) 956-9968/ management@iskconhouston.org

Kansas City, Missouri – 5201 Paseo Blvd./ Tel. (816) 924-5619/ Fax: (816) 924-5640/ rvc@rvc.edu

Laguna Beach, California – 285 Legion St., 92651/ Tel. (949) 494-7029/ info@lagunatemple.com

Las Vegas, Nevada – Govinda's Center of Vedic India, 6380 S. Eastern Ave., Suite 8, 89120/ Tel. 702) 434-8332/ info@govindascenter.com

◆ **Los Angeles, California** – 3764 Watseka Ave., 90034/ Tel. (310) 836-2676/ Fax: (310) 839-2715/ membership@harekrishnala.com

◆ **Miami, Florida** – 3220 Virginia St., 33133 (mail: 3109 Grand Ave. #491, Coconut Grove, FL

Many temples have their own websites, which you can find at: **http://directory.krishna.com**. Telephone numbers include country codes, identified by a +. To save space, we've skipped the codes for North America (1) and India (91).

◆ Temples with restaurants or dining

33133)/ Tel. (305) 442-7218/ devotionalservice@iskcon-miami.org
New Orleans, Louisiana — 2936 Esplanade Ave., 70119/ Tel. (504) 304-0032 (office) or (504) 638-3244/ iskcon.new.orleans@pamho.net
♦ **New York, New York** — 305 Schermerhorn St., Brooklyn 11217/ Tel. (718) 855-6714/ Fax: (718) 875-6127/ ramabhadra@aol.com
New York, New York — 26 Second Ave., 10003/ Tel. (212) 253-6182/ krishnanyc@gmail.com
Orlando, Florida — 2651 Rouse Rd., 32817/ Tel. (407) 257-3865/ info@iskconorlando.com
Philadelphia, Pennsylvania — 41 West Allens Lane, 19119/ Tel. (215) 247-4600/ Fax: (215) 247-8702/ savecows@aol.com
♦ **Philadelphia, Pennsylvania** — 1408 South St., 19146/ Tel. (215) 985-9303/ savecows@aol.com
Phoenix, Arizona — 100 S. Weber Dr., Chandler, 85226/ Tel. (480) 705-4900/ Fax: (480) 705-4901/ svgd108@yahoo.com
Portland, Oregon — 2095 NW Alocleck Dr., Suites 1107 & 1109, Hillsboro 97124/ Tel. (503) 439-9117/ info@iskconportland.com
St. Augustine, Florida — 3001 First St., 32084/ Tel. & fax: (904) 819-0221/ vasudeva108@gmail.com
♦ **St. Louis, Missouri** — 3926 Lindell Blvd., 63108/ Tel. (314) 535-8085 or 534-1708/ Fax: (314) 535-0672/ rpsdas@gmail.com
San Antonio, Texas — 6772 Oxford Trace, 78240/ Tel. (210) 401-6576/ aadasa@gmail.com
♦ **San Diego, California** — 1030 Grand Ave., Pacific Beach 92109/ Tel. (310) 895-0104/ Fax: (858) 483-0941/ krishna.sandiego@gmail.com
San Jose, California — 951 S. Bascom Ave., 95128/ Tel. (408) 293-4959/ iskconsanjose@yahoo.com
Seattle, Washington — 1420 228th Ave. S.E., Sammamish 98075/ Tel. (425) 246-8436/ Fax: (425) 868-8928/ info@vedicculturalcenter.org
♦ **Spanish Fork, Utah** — Krishna Temple Project & KHQN Radio, 8628 S. State Rd., 84660/ Tel. (801) 798-3559/ Fax: (810) 798-9121/ carudas@earthlink.net
Tallahassee, Florida — 1323 Nylic St., 32304/ Tel. & fax: (850) 224-3803/ darudas@gmail.com
Towaco, New Jersey — 100 Jacksonville Rd. (mail: P.O. Box 109), 07082/ Tel. & fax: (973) 299-0970/ newjersey@iskcon.net
♦ **Tucson, Arizona** — 711 E. Blacklidge Dr., 85719/ Tel. (520) 792-0630/ Fax: (520) 791-0906/ tucphx@cs.com
Washington, D.C. — 10310 Oaklyn Dr., Potomac, Maryland 20854/ Tel. (301) 299-2100/ Fax: (301) 299-5025/ ad@pamho.net

RURAL COMMUNITIES

♦ **Alachua, Florida** (New Raman Reti) — 17306 N.W. 112th Blvd., 32615 (mail: P.O. Box 819, 32616)/ Tel. (386) 462-2017/ Fax: (386) 462-2641/ alachuatemple@gmail.com
Carriere, Mississippi (New Talavan) — 31492 Anner Road, 39426/ Tel. (601) 749-9460 or 799-1354/ Fax: (601) 799-2924/ talavan@hughes.net
Gurabo, Puerto Rico (New Govardhana Hill) — Carr. 181, Km. 16.3, Bo. Santa Rita, Gurabo (mail: HC-01, Box 8440, Gurabo, PR 00778)/ Tel. (787) 367-3530 or (787) 737-1722/ manonath@gmail.com
Hillsborough, North Carolina (New Goloka) — 1032 Dimmocks Mill Rd., 27278/ Tel. (919) 732-6492/ bkgoswami@earthlink.net
♦ **Moundsville, West Virginia (New Vrindaban)** — R.D. No. 1, Box 319, Hare Krishna Ridge, 26041/ Tel. (304) 843-1600; Visitors, (304) 845-5905/ mail@newvrindaban.com
Mulberry, Tennessee (Murari-sevaka) — 532 Murari Lane, 37359 (mail: P.O. Box 108, Lynchburg, TN 37352)/ Tel. (931) 227-6156/ Tel. & fax: (931) 759-6888/ murari_sevaka@yahoo.com
Port Royal, Pennsylvania (Gita Nagari) — 534 Gita Nagari Rd./ Tel. (717) 527-4101/ dhruva.bts@pamho.net
Sandy Ridge, North Carolina — Prabhupada Village, 1283 Prabhupada Rd., 27046/ Tel. (336) 593-9888/ madanmohanmohinni@yahoo.com

ADDITIONAL RESTAURANTS

Hato Rey, Puerto Rico — Tamal Krishna's Veggie Garden, 131 Eleanor Roosevelt, 00918/ Tel. (787) 754-6959/ Fax: (787) 756-7769/ tkveggiegarden@aol.com
Seattle, Washington — My Sweet Lord, 5521 University Way, 98105/ Tel. (425) 643-4664

AUSTRALASIA

AUSTRALIA

Adelaide — 25 Le Hunte St. (mail: P.O. Box 114, Kilburn, SA 5084)/ Tel. & fax: +61 (8) 8359-5120/ iskconsa@tpg.com.au
Brisbane — 95 Bank Rd., Graceville (mail: P.O. Box 83, Indooroopilly), QLD 4068/ Tel. +61 (7) 3379-5455/ Fax: +61 (7) 3379-5880/ brisbane@

iskcon.org.au
Canberra – 1 Quick St., Ainslie, ACT 2602 (mail: P.O. Box 1411, Canberra, ACT 2601)/ Tel. & fax: +61 (2) 6262-6208/ iskcon@harekrishnacanberra.com
Melbourne – 197 Danks St. (mail: P.O. Box 125), Albert Park, VIC 3206/ Tel. +61 (3) 9699-5122/ Fax: +61 (3) 9690-4093/ melbourne@pamho.net
Newcastle – 28 Bull St., Mayfield, NSW 2304/ Tel. +61 (2) 4967-7000/ iskcon_newcastle@yahoo.com.au
Perth – 155–159 Canning Rd., Kalamunda (mail: P.O. Box 201 Kalamunda 6076)/ Tel. +61 (8) 6293-1519/ perth@pamho.net
Sydney – 180 Falcon St., North Sydney, NSW 2060 (mail: P.O. Box 459, Cammeray, NSW 2062)/ Tel. +61 (2) 9959-4558/ Fax: +61 (2) 9957-1893/ admin@iskcon.com.au
Sydney – Govinda's Yoga & Meditation Centre, 112 Darlinghurst Rd., Darlinghurst NSW 2010 (mail: P.O. Box 174, Kings Cross 1340)/ Tel. +61 (2) 9380-5155/ Fax: +61 (2) 9360-1736/ sita@govindas.com.au

RURAL COMMUNITIES

Bambra, VIC (New Nandagram) – 50 Seaches Outlet, off 1265 Winchelsea Deans Marsh Rd., Bambra VIC 3241/ Tel. +61 (3) 5288-7383
Cessnock, NSW (New Gokula) – Lewis Lane (Off Mount View Road, Millfield, near Cessnock [mail: P.O. Box 399, Cessnock, NSW 2325])/ Tel. +61 (2) 4998-1800/ Fax: (Sydney temple)/ iskconfarm@mac.com
Murwillumbah, NSW (New Govardhana) – Tyalgum Rd., Eungella (mail: P.O. Box 687), NSW 2484/ Tel. +61 (2) 6672-6579/ Fax: +61 (2) 6672-5498/ ajita@in.com.au

RESTAURANTS

Brisbane – Govinda's, 99 Elizabeth St., 1st Floor, QLD 4000/ Tel. +61 (7) 3210-0255
Brisbane – Krishna's Cafe, 1st Floor, 82 Vulture St., W. End, QLD 4000/ brisbane@pamho.net
Burleigh Heads – Govindas, 20 James St., Burleigh Heads, QLD 4220/ Tel. +61 (7) 5607-0782/ ajita@in.com.au
Cairns – Gaura Nitai's, 55 Spence St., Cairns, QLD/ Tel. +61 (7) 4031-2255 or (425) 725 901/ Fax: +61 (7) 4031 2256/ gauranitais@in.com.au
Maroochydore – Govinda's Vegetarian Cafe, 2/7 First Ave., QLD 4558/ Tel. +61 (7) 5451-0299
Melbourne – Crossways, 1st Floor, 123 Swanston St., VIC 3000/ Tel. +61 (3) 9650-2939
Melbourne – Gopal's, 139 Swanston St., VIC 3000/ Tel. +61 (3) 9650-1578
Newcastle – Govinda's Vegetarian Cafe, 110 King St., corner of King & Wolf Streets, NSW 2300/ Tel. +61 (2) 4929-6900 / info@govindascafe.com.au
Perth – Hare Krishna Food for Life, 200 William St., Northbridge, WA 6003/ Tel. +61 (8) 9227-1684/ iskconperth@optusnet.com.au
Sydney – Govinda's,112 Darlinghurst Rd., Darlinghurst NSW 2010/ Tel. +61 (2) 9380-5155/ sita@govindas.com.au

NEW ZEALAND

Auckland, NZ – The Loft, 1st Floor, 103 Beach Rd./ Tel. +64 (9) 3797301
Christchurch, NZ – 83 Bealey Ave. (mail: P.O. Box 25-190)/ Tel. +64 (3) 366-5174/ Fax: +64 (3) 366-1965/ iskconchch@clear.net.nz
Hamilton, NZ – 188 Maui St., RD 8, Te Rapa/ Tel. +64 (7) 850-5108/ rmaster@wave.co.nz 4229, Samabula)/ Tel. +679 331 8441/ Fax: +679 3100016/ iskconsuva@connect.com.fj
Wellington, NZ – 105 Newlands Rd., Newlands/ Tel. +64 (4) 478-4108/ info@iskconwellington.org.nz
Wellington, NZ – Gaura Yoga Centre, 1st Floor, 175 Vivian St. (mail: P.O. Box 6271, Marion Square)/ Tel. +64 (4) 801-5500/ yoga@gaurayoga.co.nz

RURAL COMMUNITY

Auckland, NZ (New Varshan) – Hwy. 28, Riverhead, next to Huapai Golf Course (mail: R.D. 2, Kumeu)/ Tel. +64 (9) 412-8075/ Fax: +64 (9) 412-7130

RESTAURANTS

Auckland, NZ – Hare Krishna Food for Life, 268 Karangahape Rd./ Tel. +64 (9) 300-7585
Wellington, NZ – Higher Taste Hare Krishna Restaurant, Old Bank Arcade, Ground Flr., Corner Customhouse, Quay & Hunter St., Wellington/ Tel. +64 (4) 472-2233/ Fax: (4) 472-2234/ highertaste@iskconwellington.org.nz

Far from a center?
Call us at: 1-800-927-4152.
Or contact us on the Internet.

http://www.krishna.com
E-mail: bbt.usa@krishna.com

The Nectar of Devotion

(Offer valid in US only.)

Take advantage of this special offer and purchase *The Nectar of Devotion: The Complete Science of Bhakti-Yoga*, for only **$9.75**. This is a savings of **25% off** the regular price. To receive this discount you must mention the following code when you place your order: NOD-NOI.

ORDER TOLL FREE 1-800-927-4152